Unwin Education Books

CLASSROOM LANGUAGE: WHAT SORT?

Unwin Education Books

Series Editor: Ivor Morrish, BD, BA, Dip.Ed. (London), BA (Bristol)

Education Since 1800   IVOR MORRISH
Moral Development   WILLIAM KAY
Physical Education for Teaching   BARBARA CHURCHER
The Background of Immigrant Children   IVOR MORRISH
Organising and Integrating the Infant Day   JOY TAYLOR
The Philosophy of Education: An Introduction   HARRY SCHOFIELD
Assessment and Testing: An Introduction   HARRY SCHOFIELD
Education: Its Nature and Purpose   M. V. C. JEFFREYS
Learning in the Primary School   KENNETH HASLAM
The Sociology of Education: An Introduction   IVOR MORRISH
Developing a Curriculum   AUDREY and HOWARD NICHOLLS
Teacher Education and Cultural Change   H. DUDLEY PLUNKETT and
    JAMES LYNCH
Reading and Writing in the First School   JOY TAYLOR
Approaches to Drama   DAVID A. MALE
Aspects of Learning   BRIAN O'CONNELL
Focus on Meaning   JOAN TOUGH
Moral Education   WILLIAM KAY
Concepts in Primary Education   JOHN E. SADLER
Moral Philosophy for Education   ROBIN BARROW
Beyond Control?   PAUL FRANCIS
Principles of Classroom Learning and Perception
    RICHARD J. MUELLER
Education and the Community   ERIC MIDWINTER
Creative Teaching   AUDREY and HOWARD NICHOLLS
The Preachers of Culture   MARGARET MATHIESON
Mental Handicap: An Introduction   DAVID EDEN
Aspects of Educational Change   IVOR MORRISH
Beyond Initial Reading   JOHN POTTS
The Foundations of Maths in the Infant School   JOY TAYLOR
Common Sense and the Curriculum   ROBIN BARROW
The Second 'R'   WILLIAM HARPIN
The Diploma Disease   RONALD DORE
The Development of Meaning   JOAN TOUGH
The Countesthorpe Experience   JOHN WATTS
The Place of Commonsense in Educational Thought   LIONEL ELVIN
Language and Teaching and Learning   HAZEL FRANCIS
Patterns of Education in the British Isles   NIGEL GRANT and
    ROBERT BELL
Philosophical Foundations for the Curriculum   ALLEN BRENT
World Faiths in Education   W. OWEN COLE
Classroom Language: What Sort?   JILL RICHARDS

Unwin Education Books
Series Editor: Ivor Morrish

Classroom Language: What Sort?

JILL RICHARDS
Senior Lecturer in Education
Worcester College of Higher Education

London
GEORGE ALLEN & UNWIN
Boston   Sydney

51237

First published in 1978

ISBN 0 04 372026 9 hardback
ISBN 0 04 372027 7 paperback

Typeset in 11 on 12 point Times by Red Lion Setters, Holborn, London
Printed in Great Britain by Biddles Ltd, Guildford, Surrey

Contents

1 Introduction   *page* 9

2 Self-Expression and Creativity
   as Language-Limiting Cults   16

3 Strengths and Weaknesses of User Language   36

4 The Language Demands of Subject Learning   67

5 Specialised Language and Concept
   Development   95

6 Some Conclusions and Recommendations   120

Bibliography   145

Index

Chapter 1

Introduction

The past half-century has seen the introduction of methods and approaches to teaching in both primary and secondary stages of education that reflect ideological, political and economic changes within our society. Because the economy is geared to industry, which in turn relies upon technological expertise, there is pressure upon the education system to provide within the school curriculum science subjects and techniques that are appropriate to scientific method. At the same time ideological trends have moved towards a stress upon the needs and rights of the individual, generating an increasing demand for creative studies, the humanities and opportunities for what could be termed 'social learning'.

The dilemma for the schools is how to respond adequately to pressures from what appear to be conflicting areas of need. Can they promote a level of literacy and numeracy to meet the requirements of modern society, and introduce scientific disciplines, while at the same time providing opportunities for self-expression and personal and social development? A neutral observer would almost certainly point out that the areas concerned are complementary rather than conflicting and that between them they cover only adequately the various aspects of human personality and intellect awaiting development. In theory, few would disagree with the observation; but in practice, when questions are raised as to the stage at which a particular learning experience should be introduced, the number of periods on the timetable that should be devoted to this activity rather than that, the amount of choice that should be given to individuals to decide for themselves the area of learning in which they wish to participate, irrespective of balance, then the 'in-fighting' may begin. The peculiar 'merits' of one subject-based learning experience are set up in opposition to similar contentions from other subject areas, and the desire to establish balance can be irretrievably lost.

Inevitably, these issues have their influence upon language, although the unconscious element in language use tends to ensure that few are aware of any change. Indeed, attempts to focus attention upon functions of language to discover the demands of school learning compared with the language demands of everyday life are relatively recent. Nor is it unexpected that there is a tendency for studies applied to education to refer to language as though it were some consistent fixed entity. It is particularly noticeable that where researchers are not linguistically well informed they tend to underestimate the importance of context or situation. This tendency is even more apparent in relation to sociologists and educationists generally and may explain why socio-linguistic notions of linguists like Fishman that postulate the need for an individual to develop different varieties of language in response to situation—i.e., a 'repertoire range'—have not obtained the popular support given to those who seek to identify characteristics of an 'ideal' variety that is adequate for all situations. It is certainly true that, in this country, educational theory and practice have been influenced more by the latter, particularly in relation to language stereotypes associated with social class. It is also clear that 'child-centred learning' has increasingly influenced language use and work in classrooms—predominantly in the primary sector, but also directly the teaching of English and indirectly the teaching of other subject areas including the sciences. A point not always fully appreciated is that the demands of newer modes and methods of learning and teaching can be rather different from those associated with traditional approaches. For example, current emphasis on individual and group work has produced a corresponding decline in the practice of teaching the class as a whole. The outcome is that children now hear much less of the teacher's language, and therefore the language models normally provided in this way are to a greater or lesser degree reduced. This has important implications for language development, which will be discussed fully at a later stage.

Group work provides opportunities for children to talk freely, and it is generally accepted that this improves their language, but we need to be aware that the language used in group situations will tend to be that which comes most readily to the participants. It may or may not be equal to the demands made upon them by the nature of the topic under discussion. If the language available to the members of the group is in some way inadequate, it is doubtful whether practice will improve it unless the inadequacy is identified and steps are taken to correct it. Furthermore, in a given period of group activity the teacher comes into contact with the language of a relatively small number of children because he will employ a mode of discourse to communicate with individuals or groups which necessarily excludes the rest of the class. Exchanges of discourse in which the teacher could be expanding sentences, offering alternative forms of language and correcting inadequacies will be heard at any one time by a very small number of children and lost to the majority.

The move towards learning by discovery has also brought its own peculiar language difficulties. It has been thought reasonable to suppose that experimental and other practical activities would reduce the reliance upon verbal explication. At first glance this appears to be the case, for descriptive language has been cut back to a degree at which at times the child receives no verbal framework whatever at the outset of the activity. This puts the onus of selection on the learner and creates for him the need to hypothesise, define and eventually report and record, as and when appropriate. Linguistically these functions require complex language forms. In particular, the hypothetical and defining modes make use of syntactic structures which are representative of advanced language development. It is therefore true to say that discovery methods may make more demands on language than traditional methods, while at the outset giving fewer guidelines, in the form of verbal explication, to help the child form a correct conception of the task.

This short consideration of the place of language in practices associated with child-centred learning serves to illustrate the point that these innovations are in their own way as dependent on language as the old so-called 'talk and chalk' methods which they seek to replace. Their success will largely depend upon whether or not effective ways are found to develop the language to meet the demands of the functions which pupils are now called upon to perform.

It is a matter for conjecture as to the degree to which the challenge has been recognised and met through existing language programmes in schools. A consideration of this question forces us to attempt to identify major practices and to examine the theories and assumptions upon which they are founded so as to clarify the issues involved in the underlying rationale. However, although such theoretical discussion is useful, we are faced also with the need to examine how they work out in practice. Where possible, the level of success should be assessed in relation to alternative practices, through identification and comparison of their respective strengths and weaknesses. Some practices are so clearly unworkable, or so highly effective, that we have no doubts about our impression of them. The difficult cases—and these are the more numerous—are those which have obvious contributions to make but also embody weaknesses which should be taken into account when assessing their value. Indeed, it would be advantageous if teachers were to gain insights into the peculiar contribution of an approach, a method, or a technique and, just as important, to know something of the associated limitations. Ignorance of either of these aspects can have an adverse effect upon the success of an innovation in terms of its effective utilisation in a language-promoting programme, and there are various ways in which this may happen.

Some teachers operating from an oversimplified understanding of the diversity of language behaviour may reject anything that does not offer 'comprehensive' stimulation—i.e., that does not have the facility for promoting language in all the functions considered essential at the stage of development of the pupils concerned. Others react in the opposite manner. Raising to the status of a full-scale cult what may be generally accepted as a useful contribution to one sector of language, they attempt to promote all language activity by way of the favoured cult.

There are also difficulties related to the clarification of concepts that are not uncommon in fields in which the terminology is still relatively unstable. Thus, the degree to which an innovation may be modified through personal interpretation of the nature and scope of its related concepts is impossible to assess.

Common to all the examples cited is a tendency to become so enthusiastic about the strengths of a particular practice that the weaknesses are not given the attention they justify. The outcome of this neglect is that weaknesses are left unmodified, and may prove sufficiently damaging to the language progress of pupils as to nullify the good effects of the practice. With this in mind, some language practices associated with two specific cults—namely, self-expression and creativity—will be examined in an attempt to evaluate their contribution to the language development of school-children in learning situations and how the valuable elements they may contain may be used to greatest effect.

Discussion of the latter point necessarily involves some consideration of the child's language in relation both to the functions it can perform successfully already and those it will be called upon to perform in future. Thus, in the chapter following the appraisal of practices some of the complex issues involved in understanding how pupils meet the language demands of the school will be raised. The discussion will employ current theoretical arguments and research evidence, taking as its foci demands, on the one hand, for greater acceptance by schools of 'user' language and, on the other, for simplification of the language of learning, specifically in pupil-teacher interaction, both of a general nature and within subject specialisms.

Appraisals of the kind that will be attempted are open to criticism on the grounds that it is a relatively simple matter to discover and expose weaknesses in particular trends and practices in schools, and impossible to offer alternatives that are not themselves almost as vulnerable. The more we know about the complex, varied and unconscious aspects of language behaviour, the more likely we are to admit that there is no convincing counter to this criticism. However, we can hope to discriminate between more effective and less effective stimuli, and to do so will involve recognition of some of the damaging pitfalls.

A useful start is to try to close the gap between the assumptions we have about language use in schools, and what actually happens. In relation to this, two major lines of investigation that provide useful evidence will be discussed. The first, involving practical studies of a large sample of lessons, identifies a range of language varieties in use in schools. These include distinctions related to teacher style and the language climate of classrooms at various stages in the educative process. As all distinctions cannot be accounted for in terms of personal characteristics of teachers and pupils, evidence from comparative studies of subject teaching will be introduced to support the contention that the language used in subject teaching takes its form in response to pressures from 'within' the subject or, more specifically, from the essential concepts and processes that comprise the subject.

The second line of investigation concerns the relationship between language and the modes of thinking a pupil is called upon to undertake in school learning. The most basic understanding of this problem is impossible without some consideration of the fundamental psychological processes involved in concept formation and attainment. This is offered in the penultimate chapter, along with research evidence that throws light upon the contribution of specialised language varieties to the attainment of mature concepts in subject learning.

The conclusions to be drawn from the presented evidence may persuade us that we know something of the range of functions that a pupil's language is called upon to perform in his school life. However, as the implications of any conclusions we form have to be interpreted and put into practice by teachers, a consideration of classroom language is incomplete if some recommendations are not offered that have been arrived at after careful weighing of the major points made in the conclusions. The final chapter is therefore given over to this task, using as a framework relevant conclusions from the Bullock Report (1974). The aim is to offer guidance to teachers by suggesting interpretations and possible applications to classroom practice of those recommendations in the Report that are concerned with the sort of language pupils need to understand and produce to operate successfully in the range of learning situations within a school.

Chapter 2

Self-Expression and Creativity as Language-Limiting Cults

THE CULT OF SELF-EXPRESSION

Characteristic thinking about the notion of self-expression is readily found in statements which have been made upon the subject, of which the following are a sample.

Writing from a social perspective, Halliday (1971) discusses language as social behaviour in the sense that as a social being man is constantly faced with behavioural choices. His range of choices is determined by his culture, while specific selections from the range of choices at his disposal are subject to the context of situation.

The implication of being able to choose from a range of options is that language can be looked upon as a form of 'behaviour potential' or, in other words, it is what a speaker is able to do. Halliday is aware that what a speaker 'can do' is not a linguistic notion, because it includes behaviour other than language behaviour. He postulates, therefore, that:

> If we are to relate the notion of 'can do' to the sentences, words and phrases that the speaker is able to construct in his language—to what he can say, in other words—then we need an intermediate step, where the behaviour potential is as it were converted into linguistic potential. This is the concept of what the speaker 'can mean'.

Thus, the behaviour potential of a speaker—what he wants to do—is realised linguistically in his meaning potential, which in turn is realised in his language system as what he can say.

Britton (1970) emphasises the self as the unseen point from which all is viewed. He says:

Expressive speech is language close to the speaker: what engages his attention is freely verbalised and as he represents his view of things, his loaded commentary upon the world, so he also presents himself.

Barnes (1971) is critical of the lack of opportunity for self-expression which is afforded children in school. He says:

> ... too many children spend too much time vaguely listening and then regurgitating: through the curriculum they should be required to use language for playing with stories or ideas, for exploring things and people and sometimes for organising thought and feeling explicitly.

Taken together, the statements cover the major concerns associated with an awareness of the need to give pupils opportunities to develop their own meanings and the language with which to express them.

But to what extent do the practices identified with the cult of self-expression meet the concerns to which they are a response? To begin to answer the question it is necessary to examine self-expression as it is interpreted by educational practitioners to see if the concept has largely retained its theoretical dimensions. First impressions would suggest that it has contracted and, indeed, to some degree become polarised around a view which appears to wish to define self-expression as the language which a pupil uses to say what he *feels* about something.

This definition approximates most nearly to Britton's statement, but there are certain crucial differences. Britton sees language close to the self—'expressive language' as he calls it—as a starting-point from which it is possible to progress gradually towards the transactional function and eventually the poetic function. He describes the transactional function as a means of getting things done, a participant role in which the utterance is an immediate means to an end outside itself, the efficient achievement of which dictates the form and organisation of the utterance. The poetic function is described as a more powerful exercise of language in the spectator role in which the utterance is an immediate end in itself—i.e., a verbal construct. In this the arrangement of the items is an inseparable part of the meaning of the utterance, and the listener is expected to pay attention to the forms of language as part of his response.

Practices in the teaching of English suggest that it is the poetic function of language (to use Britton's terminology) which has been taken as the model for self-expression. Furthermore, language-stimulation programmes in the early expressive stage appear to be geared to a progression to the poetic stage rather than to the transactional. This can be so marked as to give the impression that the transactional function of language is being left to look after itself. In the writings from which Britton's statement about expressive language is taken he warns against passing too quickly through the early expressive stage into the transactional, for fear that the self will be lost, but does not discuss the possible effect of promoting the poetic function at the expense of the transactional. It is reasonable to assume, however, that this too has its dangers, one of which may be that it upsets the natural progression of language towards that mature state in which it is a rich and adaptable instrument for use. Persistent neglect of the transactional function runs the risk of encouraging in the individual a reliance upon subjective judgement which prevents him from comprehending the value of a degree of objectivity. If this becomes habitual, it may well distort his view of reality. It may be that the relative lack of emphasis in respect of transactional functions has been responsible for the apparent lack of interest in the concept of self-expression which is contained in Halliday's statement—namely, the development within an individual of the ability to give what he 'can do' meanings which can be verbalised. There is no suggestion that this involves a certain sort of language, subject or situation. Rather, it is a process through which all our language behaviour can be channelled, whatever the particular function and at whatever stage of development.

Thus, a possible criticism of the interpretation of self-expression which appears to be in current use in the educational system can be made on two major counts. The first is that the interpretation leads to the introduction of advanced thought and language functions too early on. The second that the interpretation leaves out a great deal that should qualify for inclusion.

Justification for the criticism is based initially on the argument that persistent efforts to promote the poetic functions of language in children before they have mastered the other functions forces their attention artificially on to details of subjects which naturally they would be more likely to consider at a more advanced stage in maturity.

This is particularly true for subjects which demand understanding of the sort that arises from life experiences or an emotional response or both. Children—and, indeed, mature adults too—find the expression of such items, in speech and writing, a very difficult exercise. A reason which can be offered in part explanation is the converse of that given by Britton in advocating the expressive function as the starting-point for language—namely, because it is language close to the self. In this case it is precisely because the poetic function calls for a response which reveals the inmost self that many find it difficult to manage. One could say that it is *so* close to the self as to make the establishment of meanings something of a problem. In short, it is easier to say what we think we see, hear, believe to be true or know as a fact than to give adequate expression to the breadth and depth of what we feel. This view in no way contradicts Britton's notion of expressive language; rather, it serves to emphasise the distinction between the expressive and poetic functions—a distinction of which devotees of self-expression have sometimes appeared to be unaware.

Returning to the subject of the second criticism—namely, that too much is left out of current interpretations of self-expression—lack of awareness of the possible forms that expressive language can take may operate to reduce the range of language activity. There are those who expect that, characteristically, self-expression will contain an emotive component in relation to the self, and so may leave other expressive forms underdeveloped by not providing situations in the classroom where these can be stimulated and exercised. One example is the expressing of concrete concepts. An individual gradually builds up notions which in time constitute a mature concept. His ability to relate notions and to verbalise them internally will greatly affect his personal attainment of the concept. The breadth and depth of his concept at any stage in its growth can only be divulged to others through his ability to give expression to it. To illustrate this, the following are three responses made by 9-year-olds to the request, 'Tell me what a worm is like, so that someone who could not see or feel it would have an idea of what it was like.'

(a) 'It's long; it's brown; slimy.'
(b) 'It's brown; it has lines on it; it's long; it wriggles on the ground; there's a plain bit on it; it's slimy.'
(c) 'An earthworm is a blind creature which moves slowly; it's brown and legless and horrible and slimy; it has rings round it; one of the rings is much thicker; it has a dark line down its back; it's about five inches long.'

Examination of the statements shows differences in the number of items offered which could be taken as indicative of the level of development of the concept in each child. It could equally well be taken as an indication of each child's ability to verbalise what he knows, for the language used in (c) is more mature than that in (a) and (b). Very probably the notional and verbal aspects need to be taken into account in promoting the growth of concepts, but the important point is that a child may give the impression that he has not attained a particular concept simply because he cannot find the language to express his notions.

This is particularly pertinent to the expression of non-spontaneous concepts. Vygotsky's work in this field (1962) indicates the relationships between the two sorts of concept—which he calls spontaneous and scientific—and the words used to express them. He maintains that children acquire spontaneous concepts long before they are conscious enough of them to be able to define them in words. In contrast a scientific (non-spontaneous) concept usually starts its development with a verbal definition and its use in non-spontaneous operations—i.e., it starts its life in the child's mind at a level which a spontaneous concept reaches much later.

Vygotsky states:

In working its slow way upward, an everyday concept clears a path for the scientific and its downward development. It creates a series of structures necessary for the evolution of a concept more primitive, elementary aspects, which give it body and vitality. Scientific concepts in turn supply structures for the upward development of the child's spontaneous concepts towards consciousness and deliberate use.

He stresses that the inner tie which exists between spontaneous and scientific concepts is similar to that between the thought and the word which identify with a particular concept.

Vygotsky's findings, based as they are on a large amount of experimental investigation, give strong support for the view that developing the ability to express concepts—spontaneous and non-spontaneous—is of such importance in scholastic situations and those of everyday life that it should not be left to chance. Language programmes aimed at stimulating self-expression must be prepared to include within their scope the adequate expression by the child of the thoughts which are making their impression upon his mind during concept formation, from a relatively early age to maturity. Other areas which could be included along with a demand for more attention are: expressing perceptions, arrived at through straight observation as well as through thoughtful consideration, and expressing opinion based on factual knowledge or tentative hypothesis.

Putting together all the arguments that have been discussed in this section, the outcome is a plea for delineation of the concept of self-expression in language acquisition and development, so that it no longer tends to be limited to expressing an emotional self but becomes an umbrella for all the different kinds of expressing that an individual struggles to produce in the process of making sense of himself, his experiences and his world.

So far discussion has centred upon the effects upon practice of a limited theoretical conception of self-expression. It is now time to examine such practices as have emerged from the narrower conception in order to judge how effectively they achieve the objectives for which they are designed. The most popular methods used for promoting self-expression involve small and large group discussion. The actual stimuli employed to start off discussion are very varied and appear to cover an extensive range of expressive language. Examples are: materials brought into the classroom (objects, animals, charts, plants, etc.), films, topical events, poetry, drama, controversial issues, outside visits, sport, experiments, music, painting and craftwork of all sorts. The list, which is not exhaustive, gives opportunities for expressing ideas, concrete notions, emotional responses, observations, factual knowledge, hypothetical argument, emotional and logical interpretations, sense experiences and aesthetic appreciation. But are the opportunities being fully exploited? Doubtless different answers would be given to this question. One that could be given is that exploitation falls short of what it might be for two major reasons. These are: lack of balance in the selection of stimuli, and a tendency to use the same techniques for all topics—the latter being a phenomenon associated with the manner of teaching as well as the method.

Unbalanced selection of stimuli may occur at any stage in our educational system. Broadly, this refers to the habitual selection of stimuli from one sector of the available range and leads to the exclusion of other sectors which contain stimuli possessed of characteristics different from those of the favoured sector. For example, at primary level the favoured sector could well be one containing the so-called creative activities (drama, painting, craftwork), while in secondary schools in recent years a popular choice has been attitudes and values in relation to social problems or controversial issues. Lack of balance of this sort has certain potential dangers. The favoured sectors are often those to which the teacher has a commitment—albeit an unconscious one—which greatly increases the possibility of his exerting undue influence on pupil thought. Only some of the pupils in the class or group will at any one time be genuinely interested in a selected stimulus enough to wish to talk about it. Others, for reasons such as lack of interest, understanding and readiness, or temperamental difference, or just not being in the mood, will remain unstimulated. The chances of this happening repeatedly to the same pupils are much greater when selections are made from a limited sector of related stimuli.

The tendency to use the same techniques for promoting and conducting discussion shows itself in some distinctive forms: adherence to a specific preference to the rejection of other techniques, even when it is possible to demonstrate their undoubted advantage; use of certain patterns of prompting and questioning in association with a kind of neutrality that may be eminently suitable for the expression of subjective opinion off the top of the head, but which, as a technique for drawing out responses of an accurate or deeply interpretative nature, lacks a necessary sharpness and sensitivity. Two illustrations which follow serve to make clear how the limitations operate against effective achievement of objectives. They also show how opportunities for furthering self-expression, in the wider sense of the concept, are being lost.

The first instance involves discussion by a large group of teachers of English from primary and secondary schools of a film about rubbish collection, disposal, and re-cycling. The film, a colourful documentary, is intended for use in language-stimulation programmes with children within an age-range of about 8 to 12 years. A sizeable proportion of the teachers taking part made condemnatory statements about the film which were aimed not at its content or organisation but at the film as a technique. They claimed that it could not offer children first-hand experience. In their view a visit to a rubbish-disposal works would have given the children 'so much more'.

On being pressed to say to what the 'more' referred, atmosphere, feeling part of what was going on, and personal sense experience were identified. Few would wish to argue against the value to the individual of these experiences, but it does not follow that children will acquire them simply by being exposed to first-hand stimuli. Teachers who have taken classes on visits to factories and other places of interest will know something about the disadvantages of this type of activity. There may be disappointment caused by inability to see processes clearly—as in the interest of their safety children are kept well away from moving parts—and lack of understanding as explanations are drowned in background noise, ultimately producing boredom which neutralises the stimulating influence of the novel environment.

Obviously the film overcame all the disadvantages mentioned, giving close-up views of machines at work and furnaces melting metal. As an *alternative* to first-hand experience it had much to commend it. It had also certain other qualities which could have been used to advantage in the exercise of language suitable for expressing spontaneous and even non-spontaneous concepts. These issues were taken up with the group of teachers who initially had shown antagonism to the film, but they remained unconvinced that the film had any merit as a technique for promoting genuine expressive language.

There can be little doubt that stances of this kind indicate lack of balance in those who take them up. In this example teachers are prepared to exclude a method of stimulating language because it does not possess the one particular characteristic which would make it acceptable to them—namely, that of being a first-hand experience. The arguments used in support of first-hand experience reveal their preoccupation with the stimulation of a certain brand of self-expression which clearly they believe must be an emotional response for it to have real value for the child.

The second example is one of several which could have been used in which expressive language is promoted through discussion of poetry. A small class of 13-year-old pupils of above-average ability are discussing a poem which immediately prior to the discussion they have read silently from individual copies. The poem is about a boy who has climbed to the top of a tall tree in a high wind and is swinging dangerously in the slender branches.

Teacher: Shall we discuss what the boy feels like when he's up there?

Pupil 1: He must feel better than it is here. (*Laughter*)

Pupil 2: You can hardly do anything here. (*Some talk among several pupils at once, which cannot be heard clearly on the tape*)

Pupil 3: He'd be like frightened cos eh he could be thrown to the ground.

Pupil 1: He must enjoy fear though, ye know.

Teacher: Do you think he's enjoying it more than being afraid?

Pupil 1: Yes, I do, I think he's enjoying the fear.

Teacher: How would you feel yourself?

Pupils: Frightened.

Pupil 4: I think I might have gone up when the wind had stopped.

Pupil 1: He knows it's a windy day but he goes up cos it's something he wants to do.

Pupil 5: The tree would sway and that would scare him.

Pupil 3: It would be worse near the top.

Teacher: Do you think it's just something he does because it gives him a thrill?

Pupils: Yes. (*Pupils talk all at once—nothing can be heard clearly on the tape*)

Pupil 5: It's like children sliding down the roof of a shed.

Pupil 6: Yes, for fun.

Pupil 3: It's like when you're free to do anything.

Teacher: What do you get at the end?

Pupil 1: I was really glad, in a way, when he got down.

Pupil 4: I would feel glad to get down.

Teacher: What about his feelings as he lands?

Pupil 2: He doesn't really say anything.

Pupil 7: Just walks away.

Pupil 8: He's been in a sort of dream world.

Teacher: Did you like the poem?
Pupils: Yes. (*Said by several pupils together*)
Teacher: Do you think you got the feel of the poem?
Pupil 1:   It was (*doubtfully*) quite creepy.
Teacher: Anything else anyone wants to say?

No other comments were offered by the pupils, and the lesson ended a few minutes later without further reference to the poem.

How valuable is discussion on these lines for the development of self-expression within the poetic function of language? In the example a number of the pupils have picked up something of the atmosphere of the poem but, with one exception, failed to make convincing contact with the poet's meaning. They recognised the dangerous and what they called the enjoyable aspects of the boy's activities. They apparently did not sense, and certainly failed to express, the highly excitatory state which the boy induces in himself by deliberately taking a risk which could end in his death or injury. They also missed the sharply contrasting sense of quiet which descends upon the boy when, having reached the climax of his excitement, he regains his tranquillity and willingly, almost gratefully, returns to the safety of ordinary everyday life.

Why did most pupils fail to interpret the poem fully? How was Pupil 1, who was on the right track, prevented from developing his interpretation convincingly? Why did the pupils use such limited language to express their own feelings? The answers to these questions are undoubtedly associated with particular limitations of the discussion technique—namely, its failure to encourage the following-up of promising leads in order to expose meanings and to draw the attention of the pupils to the text. The former limitation loses for Pupil 1 the satisfaction of teasing out the poet's meaning and exposing it for the other pupils to their greater gain. The latter robs all pupils of opportunities for practising the use of new language forms and lexical items which can help them realise both meaning and verbal potential. By digging down into the text they can discover what the poet means and how he uses language to express his meanings. The development of their own expressive language will thus be helped if they are encouraged to take note of its expert use and try it out in their own utterances.

The examples described, which are common enough in the teaching of English today, suggest that the attention being directed at expressive language is failing to produce positive results because the popular manner of teaching shows an obsessive preoccupation with so-called democracy, neutrality and permissiveness. Support for this contention is to be found in a critical article by Robert Nisbet (1973), himself a teacher of English, in which he pinpoints some of the weaknesses of these preoccupations, exposing their effect and offering correctives. The gist of his argument is contained in the following extract from the article:

The most prominent idea in poetry teaching for years has been that a poem is something to be experienced, not taught. Analysis of any kind is felt to be hostile to the essential enjoyment on the pupil's part. Coupled with this is the idea that responses to a particular poem will vary, and it is an act of temerity on the teacher's part to dictate as to what the 'correct' response should be and that any response on the pupil's part, representing his own personal reaction, is a valid one. Herein lies the danger.

One particular concrete example always strikes me, from an occasion when I was teaching Auden's *Lullaby* to an 'O' level form. The poem's central dilemma is present in the opening lines:

Lay your sleeping head, my love,
Human on my faithless arm.

The gentle and lulling effect of the opening line is brought to a jarring halt by the word 'faithless' and the poem proceeds to address itself to the problem of reconciliation to a love which is human and fallible.

The group of pupils in question, set earlier to read the poem for themselves, had missed this point completely. They had read the poem entirely as a prettily romantic

51237

little love song and seemed somewhat exasperated by my insistence on pointing to (for example) the precise effect of the word 'faithless' in the lines quoted and its effect, in turn, on the word 'human'. They felt that this 'spoiled' the poem. Should I therefore have decided that theirs was a 'valid response' and let it stand?

Surely not. It was, obviously, a superficial response. More to the point, there is an important sense in which it was not a response to the poem at all. Their minds had a ready-made stock of romantic clichés and pre-conceived notions and they were feeding off the poem in order to reinforce them. Equally vitally, in responding as they were, they were not learning anything. In fact, it is just this sort of romantic pre-conception about love which the poem is, among other things, challenging. If this class *were* to learn anything from the poem, they would have to open their minds to the possibility of fresh, previously unthought-of responses.

This point is the essential one generally. A pupil, left to respond to a poem without guidance, is only too likely to find in the poem what he feels about its subject already, and what he wants to feel. It is our job, when necessary, to guide him towards a response which *is* a response, in other words represents a direct reaction to the poem which is being studied.

Nisbet's argument for the establishment of valid meanings is equally efficacious in relation to the establishment of appropriate language. In short, if pupils are to learn anything about expressive language from their discussion of various stimuli, they will have to have their minds opened up to the possibility of fresh, previously unthought of, varieties of language.

The examples offered appear to demonstrate a common inability to shed habitual attitudes and pre-conceived notions and look openly at the piece of language with the aim of discovering the message the writer is trying to convey. Failure to respond to the semantic clues embodied in the text implies failure to take account of the language of the writer. Thus, subtle syntactic constructions, unusual collocations of words, powerful use of idiom, to mention but a few linguistic features, may remain unnoticed, denying the reader valuable insights into the way the writer uses language to achieve his ends. These same insights can, gradually and to some degree unconsciously, enlighten readers' attempts to express themselves more adequately as they mature.

Clearly, self-expression is a necessary and natural phenomenon of language behaviour that should be given every opportunity to develop, but, like certain other similar phenomena—for example, creativity, which will be discussed next—it has been subjected at times to overemphasis, too narrow interpretation and misunderstanding of its very nature. The result has been the production of language-limiting cults, reinforcing what already exists and failing to promote diversification and extension of language into new contexts.

THE CREATIVE URGE

The thinking and motivation behind the desire to give pupils opportunities to use language creatively has much in common with the cult of self-expression. Both adopt a child-centred approach, place emphasis on first-hand experience, employ group discussion to a considerable degree and face similar difficulties. Creativity also involves 'playing' with language in order to find fresh ways of saying things, and thus demands of an individual good language resources which can be called upon as and when required. The major purpose of such activity is to awaken in children a realisation that their own language can be used in roles other than those which demand conformity to a special language system, such as scientific English, public address and the exchange of pleasantries. In other words, they can legitimately make language do what they want it to do in any appropriate context.

Drama is a medium used to encourage experimentation. For example, children are given opportunities to extemporise a dramatic situation or the words of a play with a well-known plot, having complete freedom in the choice of language.

More often, and from quite early on, there is a tendency to concentrate upon the written medium through the encouragement of what is called 'creative writing'. As in the case of self-expression, the term does not carry a clear meaning, and to understand the concept it is necessary to examine the activity to which it is applied.

The notion of creativity has always been difficult to clarify in relation to intellectual activity. A creative act, according to the dictionary definition, is one which brings something into existence, gives rise to something, originates. Hence one would expect the product of such an act to be unique, new and original. Can this criterion usefully be applied to the products of creative writing? Teachers hoping to stimulate their pupils into the production of new and original pieces of writing presumably think it can. Differences of opinion which exist are over what qualifies as a new original creative piece of writing.

One such divisive issue concerns the standpoint from which judgement of originality will be made. Must the piece of writing stand the test of public originality, of being deemed a new creation which no one has produced before, or does it qualify if it satisfies the condition of being a new creation for the individual?

Of the two, the former embodies a greater number of difficulties. It could be argued that it is not possible for an individual to decide whether or not an item of writing is original in the public sense, because his judgement is subject to the limitations of the knowledge he has of what has been written by others. Judgements may be influenced unconsciously by personal preferences for particular writers, for the notions an individual forms concerning the nature of creative language will to a marked degree reflect characteristics of style admired in works of writers which have for him a special appeal. These factors may influence teachers' judgements. For example, they may save their highest creativity-rating for the most 'outlandish' forms of writing, or look for the characteristic in the writing which approximates most closely to their own notion of creativity.

Both practices tend to narrow the field in which the pupil

is expected to operate. There is also evidence to suggest that pupils themselves become aware of these preferences. Some may decide that it is in their own interest to produce what is expected and, indeed, may be able to do this quite successfully. Presumably this would not earn the approval of teachers who wish creative writing to be something which can be said to come out of the pupil's own experience. The danger lies in the possibility that the one cannot be easily distinguished from the other—with all that that implies. Alternatively pupils may become disheartened when, in spite of all their efforts, they fail to emulate the desired style and in consequence tend to obtain the lower grades for their writings. In discussions of language use with pupils they frequently volunteer information which illustrates this point. An example which is typical occurred in a lesson which was being taped at the time and is reproduced below:

Teacher: Most of you got the right idea about the answer to question . . . er . . . six . . . but you didn't express your answer very well . . . you were vague and, um, inaccurate. . . . Paul Wilson's was the exception. . . . You wrote a very clear answer, Paul. . . . Are you good at English?

Pupil: Not really, Miss. . . . I got a 'C' on my report last time.

Teacher: H'm. . . . I'm surprised. . . . You always write well for me.

Pupil: Miss . . . we don't write about things . . . about the same sort of . . . things in English. . . . We write about . . . well . . . how we feel about something . . . like violence . . . or . . . being alone . . . that sort of thing. . . . I never know what to write.

Teacher: There must be some topics that you can find . . . er . . . something to write about.

Pupil: It doesn't really make much difference . . . when I do write something . . . I, er, think I know about, Mr —— still doesn't think much of it.

It should be made clear that the comments contained in the

excerpt were not contrived. They arose spontaneously and naturally in the course of a history lesson.

In view of the difficulties involved in trying to judge creativity by a criterion of public originality, it would appear to be more feasible to use the individual as the standpoint from which to make the judgement. An obvious advantage of doing so is that teachers are in a very good position to judge the creativeness of the pupils they know, because they can follow development over a period.

Starting from the standpoint of the individual, it is also possible to consider other notions of creativity which may be helpful to our understanding of it as a concept. Halliday (1971) in an article on language in a social perspective discusses conclusions of some researchers in this field which are relevant to a consideration of the nature of creativity. He mentions Ruqaiya Hasan, who he says has pointed out that 'creativeness does not consist in producing new sentences. The newness of a sentence is quite unimportant—an unascertainable property—and "creativity" in language lies in the speaker's ability to create new meanings: to realize the potentiality of language for the indefinite extension of its resources to new contexts of situation.' Halliday goes on to cite conclusions of Katz and Fodor (1963)—namely, that 'almost every sentence uttered is uttered for the first time. Our most creative acts may be precisely among those that are realised through highly repetitive forms of behaviour.'

For Halliday, then, creativity in language is manifested in the ability of a speaker or writer to create new meanings for himself—i.e., to extend the options he has at his disposal at the semantic stage of the social-behaviour model. Thus, it follows that creativity is not achieved through the ingestion of ready-made meanings fed consciously or unconsciously by teachers for later regurgitation in a slightly changed form, or by the acquisition of a larger-than-average vocabulary or a set of unusual lexical items from which to make selections to use in extraordinary ways in pieces of language where such items would be unlikely to occur naturally.

New meanings cannot be created in a vacuum. A constant flow of new options is needed, opening up the behaviour-potential stage—i.e., increasing the scope of what the speaker wants to do. Stimuli which help to increase behaviour-potential options do not emerge from one rather than any other context and, thus, new meanings are not restricted to discussion and writing in lessons devoted to the teaching of English. Indeed, quite the opposite is the case in respect of Halliday's notion of creativity, in which an important function of the creative element in language is that it enables the speaker continually to extend the resources of language to take in new contexts of situation.

All the so-called 'school subjects' as well as the school itself (in the sense that it is a unique social situation) are involved in the expansion of behaviour potential, each offering its own particular kind of opportunity for the creation of new meanings. Those thus created will make peculiar demands upon the lexical and syntactic scope of the pupil's language and, because of contextual differences, the language options selected to express the meaning (i.e., what he 'can say') will show corresponding distinctions. For example, to express meanings acquired from a sense experience such as a poem requires a free and imaginative selection technique—i.e., the ability to select from a large range of possibilities without the constraints of the 'closed' situation, so as adequately to communicate a meaning that has been generated as much from sensory perception as from intellectual activity. On the other hand, new meanings created in a mathematical, historical or scientific context will require very different language options, for the major concerns will be with objectivity, accuracy and conciseness of expression.

Purely social situations occur in schools which are also sources of stimulation for the increase of behaviour-potential options. The interaction of individuals with differing experiences, culture patterns and personalities calls for creativity in relation to their perceptions of each other and their evaluation of the kind of responses that are appropriate in various situations.

The notions contained in these examples are undoubtedly important for the production of suitable criteria for assessing creativeness. They suggest that the criterion of newness should be reserved for meanings and contexts. By urging the necessity of taking account of new meanings through an increasing awareness of new contexts they challenge any preoccupation with a particular creative style. By emphasising the creative nature of the internal activity which enables an individual to produce new expressions from well-used linguistic units they draw attention to the possible inadequacy of judgements which have been concerned only with the linguistic features of the end product—i.e., the piece of writing.

Without a sizeable survey it is not possible to know with any certainty whether or not teachers are aware of the issues just discussed and, if they are, to obtain a measure of their influence on practice. But there is some evidence to suggest that, although teachers quite often claim to consider the creativeness of a pupil's written work from his standpoint, in reality this usually means assessing a pupil's progress in developing language suitable for a restricted range of contexts chosen by the teacher. It rarely includes consideration of the creative activity involved in making successful incursions into new contexts which demand a totally different variety of language. It would appear, therefore, that promotion techniques and the criteria employed for assessment tend to be more suitable for fostering certain varieties of language, to the exclusion of numerous others. A piece of unprepared writing in a biology lesson produced by a boy of 14 serves to illustrate the point:

> The response to light is brought about by substances called auxins. They are produced in the buds between the leaves and are partly destroyed by light. An active auxin, or one that has not been destroyed by light, speeds the growth of plant cells. Auxins diffusing down from the shoot to the stem are destroyed on the side of the stem in light, but are not destroyed on the dark side. Consequently growth is more active on the dark side and the stem bends towards the light.

The language used in this sample shows more than mature development. The constructions used are not merely adequate;

they demonstrate the pupil's ability to create forms which are highly appropriate for the language function in which he is engaging. But would writing of this sort qualify as creative with most teachers of English? Are efforts made to develop in pupils an ability to create language to fit situations or does examination of actual practice reveal a preoccupation with two varieties—namely, modern literary language and basic conversational language? Although a good case can be made for the view that the promotion of both these varieties of language should constitute a *major* part of programmes for the teaching of English, this does not alter the fact that children need new language forms with which to respond to new demands. A great many of the practical demands which they meet cannot be satisfied adequately by the use of modern literary language or basic conversational language. Furthermore, basic conversational language starts, and often continues, as a very limited instrument for expression and communication; it becomes enriched and thus more adaptable by the absorption into itself of elements from other language forms which have been generated to meet special demands.

If much of the adverse criticism which has been directed at the creative urge appears to have as its goal the limitations of currently held concepts of creativeness, it is because these limitations influence programmes, methods of promotion and assessment criteria with subsequent consequences for effectiveness. They question the time spent trying to develop a small area of language in children who may not have developed adequate language resources or an awareness of appropriateness—i.e., choosing the right variety of language to fit the situation.

The plea is that, as the production of most language requires creative activity on the part of the pupil, 'free' use of language should not be given a position of such centrality that other sorts of creativeness are crowded out. It is also argued that what is envisaged as free use of language in creative writing can be developed effectively only from basic language resources. Otherwise it is like asking a child to compose his own cadenza when he is just beginning to learn to play his instrument.

Chapter 3

Strengths and Weaknesses of User Language

USER LANGUAGE

In discussing 'user' language it is necessary to separate the so-called 'codes' from dialects in order to appreciate the distinctions that exist in relation to their respective characteristics and limitations. Furthermore, certain conclusions formed from evidence compiled by researchers in one sphere appear to conflict with conclusions arrived at by researchers in the other sphere.

In England it is 'code users' who have been the major concern of socio-linguistic studies applied to education, largely in response to the work of Basil Bernstein.

1 *Code Users*

It is not an easy task to present a summary of Bernstein's theories, for over the past decade he has shifted his position within the same basic framework without making explicit the logical arguments or the evidence that make necessary the changes. This causes some confusion to anyone trying to understand the exact nature of the concepts used in a piece of research described in a particular paper. Certainly it is necessary to take careful note of the date on which a paper was first written, for Bernstein cannot be blamed for statements about his work made by others who are not aware of the modifications and changes which he has made over the period of a decade.

Bernstein's (1972a) premise is that forms of socialisation have the effect of orienting the child towards speech codes which control his access to relatively context-tied or relatively context-independent meanings.

Thus he argues that:

elaborated codes orient their users towards universalistic meanings whereas restricted codes orient, sensitize, their users to particularistic meanings: that the linguistic-realization of the two orders are different and so are the social relationships which realize them.

'Restricted code' is the expression he uses for the language of the working class. This he considers has a fundamentally different use of lexis and grammatical system from that of the language used by the middle class. The language of the middle class he considers to be associated with what he refers to as an 'elaborated code'.

Before discussing the characteristics of the two codes it is helpful to an understanding of their distinctions to examine Bernstein's notions of how they arise. As has been said, he attributes their character to socialisation or the process whereby the biological is changed into the cultural being. He sees this process as one of control that can evoke a particular moral cognitive and emotional awareness in a child and give it a specific form and content. He contends that the two classes employ different kinds of socialisation to a degree that produces two distinct cultures. As the child identifies with his own cultural background it influences his concept-ualisation and the manner in which he expresses himself. Thus, he acquires the speech forms or codes that go with his class.

As in the early years the main socialising agency is the family, Bernstein has concentrated his attention on language use there. He has studied the use of the mother's language for purposes of explanation, control and willingness to respond to questions and comments initiated by the child, using samples from both the middle class and the working class. He affirms that, according to the mothers' reports, there is little doubt that the two classes differ radically in their use of language for these purposes. Much of the working-class mother's communication fails to expand or stimulate the child's language or encourage him to reason things out and make tentative propositions. In short, there is a lack of openness of communication between mother and child which gives the child a narrow insular view of the world and shapes his speech acts into a restricted form that only works effectively within groups that have acquired the same code. The communication of the middle-class mother encourages an open and more flexible use of thought and language; thus, the child's view of his position in the world, and his speech acts are less tied to a given or local structure. Thus, in contrast to the elaborated-code user, the restricted-code user is attempting to express himself through a language form that is too limited, narrow and inflexible for general use.

By equating restricted code with the working class the implication is that well over half the children in state schools are experiencing a degree of language failure. However, as teachers working in predominantly working-class areas will know, this is a gross overstatement; and, indeed, we find that what Bernstein refers to as the working class is the *unskilled* working class. This is the group upon which most of his work has been concentrated and which he maintains comprises 29 per cent of the total population. The proportion is still very large. We can accept the estimation as reliable if we can also accept the notion that all persons placed in an occupational category on the grounds of a single attribute—i.e., 'unskilled'—must needs share a common cultural heritage that makes them restricted-code users. In fact, a group categorised around an attribute as general as 'unskilled' in addition to those who have limited capabilities which exclude them from semi-skilled and skilled jobs will contain those who have never had a proper job since leaving school, those who can only manage unskilled work because of some physical disability, those who are unable to find work for which they have had some training in the area in which they choose to live and thus are working below their potential and, finally, a relatively large number of women who, though capable of being trained for skilled jobs, for some reason, often domestic, accept whatever work is readily available.

As the primary object of the discussion is to expose the

strengths and limitations of 'user' language, for the present we will leave aside questions relating to definitions of social class and examine the linguistic features of the codes. A summary of Bernstein's (1971)* definitions and description of the characteristics are given below:

1 The codes are defined at the linguistic level in terms of predicting for a speaker the syntactic elements which he will use to organise meaning. For the restricted-code user the alternatives are limited, thus making it highly predictable. In the case of the elaborated code the range of alternatives is extensive; thus, the code is highly flexible and has low predictability.

An analysis of lexical and simple grammatical features carried out on samples of middle-class and working-class speech identified the following distinctions:

Group A
Middle-class groups used a high proportion of the
  following:
Subordinations
Complex verbal stems
Passive voice
Total adjectives
Uncommon adjectives
Uncommon adverbs
Uncommon conjunctions
Egocentric sequences
'Of' as a proportion of the sum of the prepositions
  'of', 'in' and 'into' (this finding is not consistent
within the working-class group)
'I' as a proportion of all personal pronouns
'I' as a proportion of total number of words
'I' as a proportion of total selected pronouns
Group B
The working-class groups used a higher proportion

---

* The original paper is 'A Public Language'. The reference given is the book containing a collection of Bernstein's papers, the original dates of which vary with the specific paper.

of the following:

Total personal pronouns

Total selected personal pronouns

'You' and 'they' combined as a proportion of total personal pronouns

'You' and 'they' combined (total personal pronouns) as a proportion of total number of words

'You' and 'they' combined as a proportion of total selected personal pronouns

'You' and 'they' combined (selected personal pronouns) as a proportion of total number of words

Sociocentric sequences.

2 Psychologically the restricted-code user experiences considerable difficulty in expressing his intent in a verbally explicit form. The elaborated code facilitates verbalisation of intent in respect of the user's social, intellectual and emotional behaviour.

3 Restricted code is more dependent upon an extra-verbal component than elaborated code. This component refers to meanings mediated through gesture and expressive associates of words.

4 The restricted code gives rise to particularistic meanings which are context-bound. This means that principles are not made explicit and the user is limited to the immediate situation. Thus, only those who share the same speech code have access to the meaning. The elaborated code gives access to universalistic meanings which are context-free. Principles are made explicit and meanings become available to everyone.

5 The syntax of a restricted code may be learned informally and readily, while that of the elaborated code requires a much longer period of formal and informal learning.

Our examination of the major items in the summary begins with what Bernstein refers to as the 'linguistic level' of the codes. In fact, the linguistic framework is obscure and does not qualify as a systematic analytical model able to take account of all the dimensions involved in the task of identifying and describing the language forms. Furthermore, in the absence of a theoretical foundation in which some justification is offered for features chosen as indicators of restriction and elaboration, the role of a particular feature as an inhibitor or facilitator is a matter for conjecture and is much influenced by what the user is trying to do with his language at the time. For instance, the 'high predictability' that Bernstein identifies as characteristic of the speech of restricted-code users is shared by a number of other language varieties that in other respects employ many of the features that he associates with the elaborated code. An example is legal discourse, which, conforming to the constraints imposed by the need to be unambiguous, accurate and objective, makes use of highly predictable lexical and syntactic items.

In view of the magnitude of Bernstein's claims, and the extent to which they appear to have been accepted, it may come as something of a surprise to find that both groups use the same linguistic features in their language but in different proportions—i.e., the distinctions identified come down to being a matter of degree. However, to understand how and why the distinction is of such importance a more precise explanation of the phrase 'use a higher proportion of' is needed as well as information about the contexts in which a feature is used appropriately or inappropriately.

At the psychological level further weaknesses are revealed. Bernstein uses hesitation phenomena and rate of speaking as indicators of the quality of verbal planning, citing the work of Goldman-Eisler (1961) as support. In the case of the former indicator he interprets Goldman-Eisler's work erroneously, confusing lexical information with structural organisation, thus invalidating this part of his 'proof'. In the second case Bernstein equates the slower speech of the middle class with a higher level of verbal planning, presumably because Goldman-Eisler found that when a speaker switches from description to abstraction there is a marked slowing-up in the speech rate. What Bernstein fails to take into account is that she also observed considerable differences among individuals in their speech rate, which were attributable to personal characteristics. Her conclusions in 1965 were that it seems likely 'that characteristic dispositions to pausing in speech could obscure any relationship that might exist between the quality of generalisation and pause time'. These conclusions leave very little evidence to support the contention that the quality of verbal planning is higher in the speech of middle-class children.

Coulthard (1969), discussing restricted and elaborated codes, draws attention to the fact that Bernstein's indicators of the level of verbal planning are founded on the assumption that an explicit meaning requires a high level of structural organisation and lexical selection, while a group-held idea will be expressed in frequently used, ready-formed phrases which reduce the level of verbal planning. Although this *may* be the case, there is in fact no inherent reason why it should be so. Hence the assumption should be looked upon as hypothetical, especially as Bernstein offers no examples of the stereotypes, so as to enable them to be set beside the examples of Chomsky, who contends that most sentences are unique.

In discussing items 3 and 4 of the summary it is essential to explore the role of context, for clearly any limitations characteristic of one or other code will occur in respect of specific contexts. This can be undertaken more readily if initially the links that Bernstein makes between code and social class are ignored. The features presented as characteristic of the respective codes will then be discussed along the dimension of style of discourse and in relation to certain defined contexts.

The restricted code contains many features that are present in the style or discourse typical of language varieties in use among intimates of various kinds like the family, friends and fellow-enthusiasts for some interest or activity. In such varieties the language is appropriately personal, colloquial and in certain respects syntactically simple. Familiar terms and phrases are much in evidence, and meanings are often mediated through gesture and expressive associates of words. In accord with Bernstein's conclusions about the restricted code in item 5 of the summary, the syntax of these varieties is learned informally—indeed, unconsciously—through usage and should therefore present no problems to a user, whatever his social class.

At this point we can see why Bernstein found it necessary to modify his early view that a restricted code is typical only of working-class groups. Unfortunately, his later admission that middle-class groups do use restricted codes did not go far enough to remove the erroneous belief that has dominated the educational scene for so long: that working-class speech is inadequate in general terms. The fact of the matter is that everyday life provides many contexts in which restricted codes are entirely adequate and, while it is true that the range depends upon personal life-style, we cannot assume automatically that this will favour middle-class users. Fishman (1970) makes an important statement on this point. Writing in a work on socio-linguistics he says:

> As long as individuals in each class can differ in repertoire, depending on their personal opportunities and experience, with respect to interaction with various speech networks, there can be no complete freezing of social class position, and no overriding alienation into separate religious, ethnic or other relatively fixed and immutable speech communities.

Within the context of the school it is unlikely that users will have any real problems in relation to varieties associated with restricted code as the evidence, including Bernstein's, points to these as being readily acquired when necessary. Thus, allegations that working-class children are alienated from school because they cannot understand the ordinary every-day language of their teachers appears to be a gross exaggeration of the truth. On the other hand, users whose language repertoires consist largely of restricted-code varieties may have difficulty in contexts where meanings have to be expressed through an elaborated-code variety. The major cause of the difficulty (as Bernstein agrees) is that users have to 'learn' elaborated-code varieties because they tend to employ linguistic features that give rise to a style of discourse which is impersonal, formal and at times highly complex. Clearly this is not the style of everyday discourse but a style much associated with specialist varieties such as scientific

English and with 'public' speech and writing.

When the occasion demands, a competent language-user should be able to operate in an appropriate elaborated-code variety. A user unable to do this could then be said to have a deficiency in the specific context in which his language fails to enable him to understand and convey messages.

The crucial question for those concerned with the limitations of code using is: Can working-class children whose language *tends* to be more dominated by restricted-code varieties than is that of their middle-class counterparts acquire and use elaborated code when the context requires it? Lawton's study (1968) of the speech of a sample of boys representative of both classes throws some light on the question. Briefly, he came to three important conclusions, which were:

1 Speech varied more according to general context of situation than according to social class.
2 There was evidence to suggest that in relation to descriptive and abstract language there were social-class differences in code switching.
3 The speech of working-class boys did not break down when they were required to switch to an elaborated code, but they obviously experienced coding difficulty.

Supportive evidence for Lawton's last conclusion comes from two studies of the present writer (Richards, 1971 and 1974). The samples of speech obtained from close on a hundred lessons contain a large number of instances of code switching by working-class children, some as young as seven years of age.

Undoubtedly some children carry out 'switching' from one code to another more readily than do others. They may have greater ability or a life-style that brings them into contact with situations in which elaborated-code varieties are in use. This will help them to acquire and employ elaborated codes for themselves, when the need arises. Such children are more likely to be members of the middle classes. However, as a child can improve his performance with the right kind of help and practice, there is no reason to suppose that the factor of class *determines* the ability to acquire or not acquire a satisfactory level of competence.

It would not be an overstatement to say that in this country Bernstein's socio-linguistic theories are not only the most widely known of any that have been offered in the past two decades, but they have also received a largely uncritical acceptance from those concerned with education, at all levels, and to a considerable degree from others of the general public. The use of the term 'uncritical' may appear harsh, but it is difficult to believe that the numerous contradictions and weaknesses, sociological, psychological and linguistic, could have passed for so long without much comment, if a careful examination of the argument and its supporting evidence had been undertaken at the outset of the work. Perhaps the theories fitted all too neatly into one or other side of controversial issues at a time when the emotional climate was right. It fits the 'nurture' side of the nature-nurture intelligence debate, the 'environmentalist school' of sociology, the political left wishing to stress the unfairness of the class system, the educational theorists anxious to blame the lack of academic success in certain groups of working-class children on something external to the policies and practices going on within the schools, and teachers themselves who see the theories as the 'simple explanation of why some children don't cope very well in school'.

On the credit side, the theories have generated a great deal of research which has and is providing new insights into our understanding of language use. It is not surprising that some of it is critical of Bernstein and, indeed, provides evidence that refutes certain of his claims. As yet the criticism has not weakened his impact significantly and no alternative has been taken up, as Coulthard (1969) puts it, 'to link a child's environment with the extent to which he falls below his potential ability'. Coulthard goes on to make the point that, until it is possible to demonstrate in detail differences between actual and potential ability (a difference he calls 'linguistic depression'), it is unlikely that any successful attempt can be made to help the linguistically deprived child.

2 *Dialect Users*

Developing from the work of researchers like Loban (1966) and Labov (1968) is a small-scale but determined pressure for increased use of appropriate dialect in pupil-teacher dialogue, primers and other language activities. It is argued that dialects are as 'good' as standard English and, indeed, that standard English is itself just another dialect. The latter point has about it a degree of illogicality in that dialects are normally considered to be deviants from a norm, and that norm is surely what is meant by standard English. Thus, it would appear impossible for standard English to be a norm and a deviant at one and the same time. A further point which needs clarification is: If standard English is just another dialect, what, then, is the norm against which other forms must have been compared to be declared dialects?

The most important reason for this interest in 'user language' is its possible influence on pupil performance in schools. Thus, in the view of the pressure groups, children would be more likely to attain satisfactory levels of achievement in school if taught in a language form familiar to their ear and tongue.

Although this view has had some influence on classroom dialogue and the language used in children's films and television programmes, it has not made much impact on the production of texts for teaching reading. It is this omission which supporters of 'user language' wish to see rectified. Much that can be said in opposition to this proposal constitutes the greater part of the case against a general increase in the use of dialect in schools.

In the first instance, arguments put forward for increasing the use of dialects are based on the contention that they are as 'good' as standard English. Labov's comment that Negro dialect is a coherent language system with its own lawfulness is frequently cited in support of the contention.

To form a judgement as to the reliability of this claim it is necessary to look at the studies undertaken by Labov (1968), in conjunction with other colleagues, of the linguistic competence of poor black children.

His sample consisted of some 200 Negro boys between the

ages of 10 and 17 years in a lower-class area of Harlem. We are told that most of the boys belonged to some sort of organisation in the community, the type of organisation varying from those organised by local government bodies to neighbourhood gangs. Additional information was obtained from middle- and lower-class Negro adults, younger boys and adolescent girls, all from the neighbourhood. Labov used this information in various ways. One such was to build up a detailed knowledge of the way of life of each individual in the sample so as to be able to avoid using interview techniques likely to inhibit the normal conversational style of a subject.

Within this framework he pursued the question of expression in logical explanation, and with examples of language obtained from a limited range of situations was able to give some account of the resulting shifts in selection of linguistic features.

Labov went to considerable lengths to obtain natural speech. He used informal group sessions in which the influence of adults was kept to a minimum and introduced into conversations topics which would be important to the subject (such as fighting with other gangs) to elicit spontaneous responses. Interviews took place in an environment in which the subject felt comfortable and not, for example, in the school, which it was feared would put constraints upon him and thus his language use.

Having obtained from the subjects in the sample a large corpus of natural speech on tape, Labov and his co-workers transcribed the tapes and analysed the transcriptions in terms of phonological and syntactic structures and in terms of function. The results of the analyses were used to make comparisons between Negro speech and standard English speech.

Before going on to examine conclusions drawn from the results of the comparison it is necessary to take account of the position adopted by Labov with regard to the identification of differences. He made the assumption that lawful rules govern Negro speech and sought to discover if features appearing in Negro speech and not in standard English do so in response to Negro speech rules, and whether or not such rules relate to rules in standard English. It is as well to keep these points in mind when considering the implications of Labov's findings, which now follow.

The first conclusion is that there are many ways in which Negro English and standard English are almost identical, particularly in the sense of being influenced by similar constraints. The differences that do exist are far outweighed by the similarities. Labov stresses the point that the differences do not indicate that Negro language is an impoverished version of standard English, but that there are elements in each that are not present in the other. Thus, on the relatively few occasions that the two forms diverge the distinctions identified are of various kinds.

Social factors influence Negro speech in much the same way as they do in other speech communities; for example, there is no single form of the dialect. Adult speakers show the greatest tendency away from Negro speech forms, while the purest forms are found among young lower-class gang-members.

On the strength of his findings Labov rejects the hypothesis that Negro language is deficient in the manner that Bernstein claims for lower-class speakers through his code theory. He insists that, although the lower-class Negro child uses a form of speech which is superficially somewhat different from standard English, it is not a form which is primitive, illogical or impoverished. In its underlying syntax it is very similar to standard English and, although lacking certain features of standard English, it contains unique uses of words and has in its deep structure a complexity that involves elaborated constructions. Contrary to the use that supporters of user language in learning often make of Labov's findings, the implications of them for the commonly held view that the failure of lower-class Negro children in school is essentially a language failure is that the view is misconceived. He concedes that there are minor problems which can be caused by structural differences, but affirms that his studies show Negro speech to be so little deviant from standard English that it cannot possibly be the root cause of massive reading failure and general poor attainment of lower-class Negro children in school.

What, then, is responsible for the failure? Labov thinks that it is partly a clash between the functions of lower-class Negro speech and the functions required at school, and partly yet another clash between lower-class black values and the ideology of the educational system. The group most influenced by the clash is the full street-gang membership, which does badly at school. The boys from the same neighbourhood who are not full gang-members tend to do as well in school as non-Negro pupils. This contention that a culture clash is involved appears on the surface to agree with the findings of Basil Bernstein. The apparent similarity of view is not sustained below the surface. Labov dismisses anything as simple as Bernstein's codes theory and opposes the notion of language deprivation in relation to Negro language. His evidence in respect of Negro speech refutes rather than supports Bernstein's notion of a lower-class culture having an impoverishing influence on the language of its members to a degree sufficient to explain their poor school-performance. Indeed, the richness of the conceptual language which Labov insists is characteristic of pure forms of Negro speech persuades him that the Negro street-gang culture makes linguistic demands upon the language of members which can be said to be essentially literary.

Labov's dismissal of poor children's language deprivation is based upon the evidence obtained from the studies just described, and in seeking to understand the implications of his conclusions for socio-linguistic studies of the language of British schoolchildren it is necessary to do so in conjunction with a critical appraisal of certain aspects of his findings.

First, much of his evidence is impressionistic, and he is guilty of choosing known speech variables to set against social variables for possible correlations. The weakness of this method is that one can expect to get positive correlations from hypotheses which have been specifically formulated to confirm hypotheses.

He affirms that the differences he identified in his analyses are so small that they cannot account for the underachievement of poor children—a view which challenges the conclusions of many linguists. Can it be assumed that in his comparison of samples of colloquial Negro speech with standard English he included features which would indicate whether or not the expected deviation could limit the speaker's capacity for using varieties of language in response to constraints and demands from situations other than informal ones? For, if we accept that the important issue for the user is not what language *is* but what it is *for*, whether or not Negro dialect is structurally as logical or as flexible as standard English—and the latter is doubtful—what really matters is what the user can do with it.

Let us look at one of the more obvious uses to which language is put—namely, for personal communication. As a means of communicating with family groups and the local community, Negro English and other dialects are unquestionably as adequate as standard English for most situations. However, there is every reason to suppose that personal communication will not be limited to these two areas, and once the subject moves outside the kinship and local community networks he may be forced to modify his dialect to be understood.

The strength of Labov's method of research is his success in creating opportunities for informal spontaneous speech by providing situations which do not inhibit the speakers and topics in which they would be naturally interested. Yet this strength can be regarded as a limiting element if considered from the standpoint of situation. It can be argued that an individual's language changes, often quite unconsciously, to fit different situations and that what Labov has contributed is a detailed account of spontaneous speech from the situations most likely to encourage the use of a highly informal variety of language. We would expect such situations to have the same sort of influence upon all speakers, especially children. As the style of such speech is highly personal and colloquial, it normally makes relatively few demands upon the linguistic competence of the user, and thus may be used for a considerable proportion of their spoken language.

The proportion of speaking-time taken up with colloquial speech will largely depend upon the number of other situations calling for language changes which confront the speaker.

Children meet such situations in school, and thus it is useful to look at Labov's evidence from the standpoint of situation. Unfortunately, the examples he cites do not throw light on whether or not he was concerned with the dimension of situation. Furthermore, as he deliberately limited the situations from which he obtained his speech samples there is little information available concerning the manner in which poor Negro children attempt to meet the speech demands of situations that included formal ones. He maintains that the boys in his sample understand standard English, and that most can produce it, but he does not tell us in what context these activities are possible.

Returning to an earlier comment on the degree of flexibility of a dialect as compared with standard English, there is little doubt that standard English is more adaptable than dialect for different contexts. The highly personal elements in dialects, arising as they do from the day-to-day dialogue of close-knit communities, are not readily modified to take account of demands for new technical vocabulary and specialised language associated with the numerous activities of modern society. English—and by implication this means standard English—enjoys a reputation for being highly flexible, with a particular talent for coining new words and phrases which are quickly absorbed into the language. Thus, there is strong evidence to suggest that dialect users will find it advantageous to avail themselves of the adaptability characteristic of standard English so that they can respond to situations which demand it.

It would seem, therefore, to their advantage to learn to do this in school, quite naturally through encounters with the language varieties provided by people and subjects. On the other hand, reinforcement of dialect—and, if we consider the enormous range of dialects in this country equable reinforcement would seem to be an impossibility anyway—may serve only to ensure that the child's area of language confidence, and thus his area of operation, is restricted to his local community. The general effect of this practice is divisive, because it is instrumental in accentuating the degree of isolation which is characteristic of small groups using language which deviates from what is accepted as being the standard form for the language community. This apparent disregard for situation as a factor exerting a strong influence on speech acts is a weakness in Labov's work. However, as situational influences generally begin to have more effect towards and during the secondary stage of education some of Labov's evidence is not affected by the omission.

Primarily, his findings still challenge the current tendency to blame inadequate language development for failure in initial reading. The points he makes about the Negro child's background being a highly verbal one appear to have convinced Rosen (1972) that something similar is true of working-class children. He uses Labov's findings in a critique of Bernstein's theories and in his conclusion writes:

> I *am* saying that the relationship between class and speech cannot be described or understood by the usual sociological methods. Working-class speech has its own strengths which the normal linguistic terminology has not been able to catch. There is no sharp dividing line between it and any other kind of speech, but infinite variations in the deployment of the resources of language.

If we accept that the language of children from all types of normal background is adequate to cope with such skills as reading, does it follow that Labov's conclusions (that educational failure is the result of a class-culture clash) afford the explanation of initial reading failure that we are seeking? There are reasons for suggesting that it does not. In the first place, Labov affirms that the Negro boys in his sample can understand and use standard English when they want to. The implication is that the boys have become aware of the existence of two cultures and in choosing one have rejected the other. Such a position would be unlikely to come about in the early years of a child's school life. Young children entering school are likely to be ignorant of the concept of culture, and gang membership would not become a serious option for several years. However, even if it were possible, through early socialisation, to bring about rejection of school values before the child arrives there, on Labov's evidence this is not the case, for he affirms that the guardians of the particular culture are the young teenagers and not the adults in the community. It would seem, then, that his conclusions may explain why at some stage in their school life certain pupils begin to fail, and why the degree of failure increases with time. What they do not give is an adequate explanation of initial problems of educability in the early stages of the primary school.

On the other hand, it is difficult to go all the way with him in respect of his statements about class values. His interpretation of the culture clash as being between the culture of the Negro street-gang and that of the middle class requires acceptance of an assumption that the exploits (drug-taking, stealing, killing, brutality, insulting behaviour, etc.) of the heroes of Negro poems and toasts violate *only* middle-class values. Labov cannot be ignorant of the knowledge that some primitive tribal societies for whom the concept of 'middle class' has no meaning live by codes which would be similarly violated by the behaviour described—not to mention the values of the vast majority of working-class Americans. It is difficult to find a convincing explanation of these discrepancies which does not foster the suspicion that the current sociological climate is one in which the notion of a culture clash will find ready and largely uncritical support, as long as one side of the clash is said to be middle-class.

This criticism is not intended to suggest that Labov's claims are without foundation. The case for the existence of a well-developed speech form is not questioned. The object of the critique is to bring to light any weaknesses which need to be taken into account when considering the implications of the work. Two weaknesses have been suggested.

First, the omission of 'situation' from criteria relating to the quality of a language form adversely affects judgements, from the aspect of language as an instrument for use. The question of whether or not Negro language can work adequately for the speaker in a variety of situations, including formal ones, remains unanswered.

Secondly, Labov's interpretation of the culture clash as

involving only the street-gang membership and the middle class does not come to terms with the core of the problem, which is that the life-style of the Negro gang-member appears basically anti-social in terms of the norms of most societies. Few viewing the culture from without will wish to join it, but a good many (Labov suggests that about half the boys in the Negro community do not join street-gangs—i.e., were 'lames') will try to escape from it. One method of escape will be through the educational opportunities afforded by the school. Thus, in this respect the school fulfils a need. The question of whether in the future schools will be able to offer something meaningful to those Negroes who at present embrace the cultural norms of the street-gang is one which is more likely to be decided by American society at large than by the education system.

The extent to which Labov's work has relevance for the British scene is a question about which views vary. There are those, like Rosen (1972), who see his work as a strong challenge to certain socio-linguistic notions that have stemmed from Basil Bernstein's code theory. Others think that the situation for lower-class Negro speech in America has a parallel in the regional dialects of this country. This belief, as has been mentioned earlier, has found expression in a tendency to talk and write about the 'quality' of dialect forms of English in words and phrases of the sort used by Labov in his description of Negro speech. What is altogether strange, bearing in mind Labov's contention that Negro language is not sufficiently different from standard English to explain educational failure, is the claim by pressure groups in this country that dialect users do experience language difficulties in school which adversely affect their performance.

It can be forcibly argued that the communities of dialect users which still exist bear little or no resemblance to the Negro ghettoes in which Labov worked. Indeed, in Britain it is difficult to find a community which has retained a distinctive life-style. The growth of towns, the development of roads and communication systems, the move from the land to the towns for work, and comparatively recently some movement back to the villages in search of more satisfactory places to live have all played their part in changing the character of what were once close-knit communities, and these changes are reflected in the speech acts. But perhaps an even greater influence is exerted by the mass media. This is now so much part of the everyday life of all people that, if the problem of a culture clash exists at all, it should be a diminishing one. Certainly, most of those who retain a dialect do so side by side with what we could term the standard English of the mass media. Indeed, the presence of television in the majority of homes, including very poor ones, has made sure that from an early age children will hear standard English spoken, accompanied by visual material which will aid understanding. It is not unlikely that in some homes children hear more language by way of the television than from their own parents. Excursions into centres for shopping, and visiting cinemas and churches, etc., will also afford opportunities for becoming acquainted with the use of standard English. Thus, the task of promoting standard English is not the mammoth undertaking it is sometimes made out to be. Nor need its practice prevent the use of dialect in communication between fellow-users and in ordinary conversations where its adequacy for conveying meaning is not in question. There are situations enough in day-to-day usage to bring into use both varieties of language, and it is a wise child who can use each appropriately.

Examples of 'isolation' are to be seen in parts of the United States of America, although it must be said that racial and cultural factors have also played their part in creating the Negro ghettoes, etc. For the remainder of dialect speakers it seems reasonable to suppose that they understand and are willing to use standard English if the situation calls for it.

The presence of a number of dialects within the language community is by no means confined to this country and the United States. Such problems as do arise are comparatively small in relation to those of countries in which the dialects are so deviant from the standard form that they almost constitute other languages; or where, within the country, more than one language is in common use. Attempts to promote dialects as alternatives to standard English can only exacerbate what problems there are. To contemplate such action in an area as small as the British Isles is altogether ludicrous.

Although Labov's work may have limited relevance in relation to dialects, much of what he has to say about the problems associated with communities like the Negro ghettoes is applicable to any group that develops a subculture which alienates it from the basic norms and values of the society at large. There is ample evidence to suggest that such groups, which may be composed of immigrants, naturals or a mixture of both, are growing up, particularly in certain areas of our larger cities. Bearing in mind Labov's findings, the solution to the problem has to be a social one, with education as one of the socialising agencies playing its part. The danger lies in believing the problem to be solely educational and thus expecting a cure to be effected through this agency alone.

3 Language of Pupils and Teachers

Not all varieties of user language can be thought of as dialects or codes. A child employing neither of these and with normal language acquisition still may be unable to manipulate his language effectively to meet all the demands made upon it by the functions he is asked to perform.

Children in school frequently come up against this problem; what they can and do produce commonly being referred to by teachers as the 'child's own language'. This expression serves a useful purpose in giving recognition to the presence of language forms that differ in some respects from those of the mature adult, but it is important that teachers do not assume that one child's 'own' language is exactly the same as that of another. We have noted earlier that differences occur that are associated with range and usage.

Although the expression the 'child's own language' is much used, it may not necessarily be taken account of. Among the issues raised by research into language use in schools is one by Barnes (1971) which highlights the possibility that it is the *language* used in learning activities rather than the thinking demanded which may exceed the child's developmental level. He calls for an awareness in teachers of the range of language possible in the classroom and the relationship of kinds of language use to kinds of learning. He maintains that there is a dominant language in use in secondary schools which he calls the 'language of secondary education' (after Rosen). This, he claims, shows common characteristics with textbooks, and other printed material that discusses a subject in a manner which is public and impersonal. Most teachers are not aware of their own language. If questioned, frequently they consider it to be simpler than it really is. Thus, they present their pupils with complex forms which they do not always attempt to simplify, because they fail to perceive the language difficulties with which their pupils are faced. In this conclusion he says:

> It seemed likely that extraneous barriers were introduced into children's learning (*a*) by linguistic forms whose function was social rather than intrinsic to the material and processes being learnt and (*b*) by unfamiliar sociolinguistic demands and constraints arising in the control system of the secondary classroom. (Barnes, 1969)

It may seem strange that the notions offered by Barnes concerning language use in the classroom should have made such an impact in view of the relatively small scale of his initial investigation. Indeed, it is misleading to suggest that he offers an original theory of any kind and, as he readily admits, his interest in classroom language as an area of inquiry initially was stimulated by an unpublished paper of Rosen. In the paper Rosen deprecates the gulf that exists between the language of the school and that of the children in it, especially in respect of the impersonal style of much of the former. It is he who suggested to Barnes the existence of a 'language of secondary education' not specific to the subjects but in his view forming a greater potential barrier to learning.

The original intention of Barnes (1969) was a 'study of the linguistic expectations set up in first year lessons in secondary schools'. He hoped that generalisations could be drawn from lessons in secondary and primary schools and set side by side for the purpose of comparison, in order to identify some of the difficulties of adjustment facing children who have just entered secondary schools. He completed the part concerned with the first year of secondary school, using tape-recordings of lessons that had been obtained, transcribed and analysed according to a scheme he supplied, by teachers studying for a Diploma in Curricula Studies at the University of Leeds Institute of Education. Having obtained the results, he decided not to pursue the study of language in the primary school, but instead to concentrate on

> the interaction between the linguistic expectations (drawn from home and primary school experience) brought by pupils to their secondary schools, and the linguistic demands set up (implicitly or explicitly) by the teachers in the classroom.

Barnes decided on a descriptive study of the lessons of 11-year-old children in the first half of the first term, with the intention of recording the whole language environment of the lessons. To do this he used material provided by the collaborating teachers in 1966 and fresh material obtained from following a first-year class through a whole day of lessons in a comprehensive school. They were hoping to obtain samples of spoken language from the teacher's exposition and questions, discussion, both teacher-initiated and pupil-initiated, interchanges in the cause of teacher-pupil and pupil-pupil relationships and other discussion between pupils.

Written samples of material used in the lesson were taken from textbooks, teachers' notes, charts, blackboard work and pupil writing both teacher-defined and pupil-defined. With one exception, the investigator was present during all the lessons and thus able to supplement the recording with information about contributions which were not clear on the tape, non-verbal behaviour, diagrams and blackboard work. It was hoped that he would also be able to provide fuller details of the proportion of pupils who spoke and for how long, but this proved virtually impossible.

Barnes takes the categories he identifies in the analyses as indications of the teacher's concept of the purpose of the lesson. As such it is highly important, for the teacher's version indicates to the pupil not only what is to be learned, but also his role as a learner in the particular subject. Barnes uses several categories which are concerned with the language used by pupils in questions, discussions and anecdotes to verbalise their learning. This function he considers central to the process of learning, and therefore considers the teacher's task to be one of helping pupils to use language to organise experience and not one of introducing a specific set of linguistic forms.

Four or five categories are included in order that an assessment of the possible language gulf between teacher and pupil may be made. These categories also show how much use is made of subject registers and the 'language of secondary education' (which has been mentioned earlier), which tends away from the normal 'conversational' language of pupils. Barnes asserts that the latter is not tied to a special subject context and in his view more often obstructs than promotes learning. Taken all together the various categories are expected to provide evidence which will determine whether or not the language in the classroom is fulfilling its function as an instrument of learning.

The teachers' questions were found to be predominantly factual. This is true in arts subjects to a degree that causes Barnes to assert that teachers of the arts subjects seem more concerned with passing on information than with stimulating thought. Science subjects have a greater proportion of reasoning questions, most of which are 'closed' because they are calling for explanation. Barnes deplores the shortage and, in some lessons, complete absence of 'open' questions and interprets the phenomenon to mean that teachers perceive their main task to be the transmission of ready-made notions and not the promotion of active participation on the part of the pupil in all language functions. He poses two questions: (*a*) should factual material predominate in arts subjects at first-year level, and (*b*) might arts and science be taught more effectively if the approach were more open-ended? There is no doubt that he means genuinely open-ended and not the pseudo-variety in which the question sounds as though it is giving choice but in fact pupils are expected to conform to an unstated criterion which severely limits the number of acceptable answers. This would, in Barnes' opinion, prevent the loss of anecdotal contributions of the sort that children bring from the primary school but cease to offer very quickly when they learn that the teacher regards them as irrelevant. Barnes (1969) hypothesises that:

> they begin to take part in each new 'subject' by taking in their teacher's behaviour as a reciprocal element of their own role as learners, so that his voice becomes one 'voice' in their own internal dialogues.

Teachers talk a great deal more in a lesson and pupils a great deal less than the former are aware. This is largely because thinking aloud by pupils in order to generate new sequences and consider implications is rarely encouraged; indeed, the teacher may cut short any verbal improvisation because it disrupts his plan of how the lesson should 'go'. This is particularly detrimental to the development of a pupil's concepts, for there is nothing to bridge the gap between his frame of reference and the teacher's. Barnes (1969) describes what happens in this situation:

> This teacher teaches within his frame of reference; the pupils learn in theirs taking in his words which 'mean' something different to them, and struggling to incorporate this meaning into their own frames of reference. The language which is an essential instrument to him is a barrier to them.

One would expect that the receipt of new information, especially if it is couched in unfamiliar language, would call forth questions from the recipients. The shortage of pupil-initiated discussion in the samples suggests that for some reason this does not happen. Nor is Barnes prepared to agree that questions are not being asked because most pupils are following the teacher's exposition with such a high degree of understanding that further enlightenment is unnecessary. The few sequences which were initiated by pupils were relevant to the learning tasks involved and included testing insights, seeking theoretical explanation and correcting errors made by the teacher. The implication of the lack of pupil-initiated questions is clearly that only a very small number of pupils are *actively* engaged in learning. It follows that, when a teacher gives no opportunities to pupils for making their meanings explicit, he is in no position to judge how far what the pupils have learned differs from what he thinks he has taught.

Barnes examines what the teacher teaches under two headings, which are: (*a*) the language of instruction and (*b*) the language used to control classroom interaction. In the case of the former, he found that specialist language was used which at times was presented to the pupils and at other times used without deliberate presentation. He contends that this awareness of some aspects of their language was common to all teachers in the sample and that equally common was their unawareness of other aspects. He supports his contention with references to the deliberate presentation of a technical term, in which the language used to make the presentation is as unfamiliar to the pupils as the original term, and to numerous examples of specialised language used without there being made any attempt to present or simplify it. Finally, he instances numerous occasions on which the language of secondary education is used, thus presenting pupils with a form of language which they would not normally use themselves or hear others use. The use of this last is a practice which attracts considerable criticism from Barnes, and he examines the language form in order to identify and describe its major characteristics.

In the first place, he identifies the form as different from specialised subject registers, and in doing so employs the categories of 'linguistic-intellectual' and 'linguistic-conventional' (after Rosen).* 'Linguistic-intellectual' refers

* H. Rosen, 'The Problems of Impersonal Language' (unpublished paper).

to language which is carrying conceptual processes and as such is a specialised register. Characteristics of such a register are the high level of agreement among users on the meaning of words and the likelihood that, once the hearer or speaker is favourably predisposed by training to respond to the register, messages, if grasped, are unmistakable.

'Linguistic-conventional' refers to a socio-cultural role in which the speaker signals to himself and others that he is no longer speaking personally but as one who has taken on a specific role—for example, that of historian, scientist or teacher of mathematics. Difficulties arise in classifying the 'language of secondary education' because, although many instances can be readily categorised as socio-cultural or conceptual, there is within socio-cultural functions no clear-cut line between the specialised registers and that of the 'language of secondary education'. It is also true that, although teachers of a specific subject specialism are aware of the conceptual function of the subject register in relation to the carrying of precise meaning, by and large the pupils do not have the same awareness and, in the view of Barnes, may receive them as though they were characteristically socio-cultural. Thus, they accept a subject register as something that is associated with how the teacher of that subject talks.

The subject registers and the register of the 'language of secondary education' played a large part in the lessons which constituted the sample used by Barnes. He considers the latter to be potentially more dangerous as a hindrance to learning because teachers are less aware of its existence than they are of subject registers. While accepting that linguistic registers may have a useful conceptual function, he deprecates their dominance in classroom language, especially in the language of the teacher. He contends that they may prevent some pupils from identifying their purposes with those of the teacher, and questions whether the language of secondary education serves any useful purpose in teaching secondary-school subjects and, if it does, how pupils can be encouraged to acquire what is necessary.

While, obviously, there are grounds for criticising the excessive complexity of the language of learning, particularly in relation to subject specialisms, there is evidence to support the contention that the extent to which this can be done is limited by other factors. Evans (1972) provides evidence from a research study concerning the contribution to the complexity of language of the technical vocabulary present in school subjects. In discussion of the possibility of simplifying school biology texts he points out that technical terms have an essential function—namely, to facilitate precise communication. The advantage of a technical vocabulary is that in a particular context each term carries one meaning. In other words, the intention is to convey one concept. A measure of the usefulness of such terms when employed in speech and textbooks is that they contribute to the formation of useful concepts. A good book and a perceptive teacher will present important terms in more than one way, illustrate where possible, discuss central concepts fully without employing large numbers of other terms which are not essential, and never use terms without explaining them. When this is not done, especially at secondary level, there are the dangers of presenting terms which do not carry meaningful concepts— even though pupils may use the terms freely—and of restricting communication by failing to identify a known concept with the correct technical term.

The difficulties associated with vocabulary are not the only ones to be tackled in the quest for simplicity. Taylor (1968), in his rigorous study of deep structure in an elementary chemistry book, comes to the conclusion that pupils will find chemistry especially difficult in the early stages, when they are unfamiliar with the combination of categories and also uncertain how to assign linguistic units to correct conceptual categories. He recommends a great deal of illustration from everyday life, but warns that this can only go so far because the learner is eventually forced back upon the purely symbolic operations of language as he tries to codify the relation between various chemistry notions. Taylor goes on to say that the relationships with which any subject discipline deals are different in a variety of ways from those of everyday life, and to learn a subject is to learn the language of the subject. For example, in the case of science subjects much of the language concerns hypothetical and ideal states, it being possible to demonstrate the relation between them only verbally. Thus, the amount of simplification possible is restricted and, while all unnecessary complication should be avoided, complex forms may be necessary to communicate concepts and notions simply, concisely and accurately. In practice there is considerable though often unconscious use of complex forms of language associated with subject specialisms, but without some sort of 'campaign' for greater consideration of the use of language in learning and teaching it is difficult to assess whether or not the balance between simplicity and necessary complexity is being achieved.

Unlike most other subject disciplines, English is to some degree exceptional in terms of possible language varieties. Although the study of language and literature can have the same problem with regard to specialised language as other subjects, teachers of English tend to have more control over what they teach, and pressure to conform to a specific language system is less powerful. Unfortunately, there is no evidence to suggest that, once free from the subject disciplines, pupils express themselves naturally in a simple straightforward way. Indeed, Labov (1972) goes as far as to say that the extent to which pupils complicate their language unnecessarily produces despair in their teachers. To take comfort from the fact that this remark is made about American pupils is to ignore the evidence of our eyes and ears that the language produced by many children in this country falls short of being simple direct English—as does the language of many adults.

In attempting to tackle the problem of confused and over-complicated language it is important to remember that a simple direct style of speaking and/or writing is not easily fostered and, indeed, may be one of the most reliable indicators of language maturity that we have. Most certainly it is not the same as basic conversational language, which tends to depend for its success on such factors as how well participants know one another and share common experiences. Simple language at its very best is able to say exactly what it wants to say in a manner which is readily understood by native English speakers.

There are teachers in primary and secondary schools who equate what they term the 'pupil's own language' with simplicity of language. It is difficult to follow their reasoning as one cannot assume that his 'own' language will be simple because he is unable to form complex constructions and use technical vocabulary. Reality can be very different. Often the language produced, though basic and repetitious in terms of lexis and syntax, lacks direction and explicitness to a degree which causes confusion and complication until the structure becomes so deviant that meaning is obscured. Acceptance of this sort of language as adequate for situations other than informal conversations removes some of the pressure on pupils and teachers to work for the development of a simple direct style of English. Thus, pupils can be left sadly unpractised in the use of a language form which is eminently suitable for adaptation in response to demands from different contexts.

The last point is of great importance in the transition from primary to secondary level. When pupils enter the secondary school they tend to be faced immediately with the specialised language of subject disciplines. If in primary school they have learned to discriminate between the loosely colloquial and the direct and simple, and to identify the occasions when it is necessary to attempt to use the latter rather than the former, they are in a good position to cope with new demands upon their language. Nor is this true only for the school situation; it gives pupils the same advantage in situations of everyday life. If, on the other hand, basic conversational English is the only well-established variety in their communicative repertoire, they will continually experience difficulty in participating in many activities and situations characteristic of a complex technical and bureaucratic society, and one such situation may well be classroom learning.

It is perhaps unfortunate that in primary schools, and in the teaching of English in secondary schools, the major interest of teachers appears to centre on the poetic function of self-expression and creativity. While this function is undoubtedly worthy of attention, and increasingly so with age, there are many quite ordinary demands which children must learn to meet with their language, so that the greater proportion of the time available for language development should be spent trying to meet those needs. The poetic function of language could then be given more prominence as basic language competence improves to the point when the child is beginning to express his meanings in simple direct English.

Chapter 4

The Language Demands of Subject Learning

In the introductory chapter it is suggested that a gap exists between what is thought to be the language used by teachers and pupils to meet the needs of learning situations and the reality of what is required and used. Initial awareness of this state of affairs was generated by responses of individual teachers and groups of teachers to questions on the subject of what they understand to be the language demands of school learning, in general terms and, if applicable, within their own subject specialism.

The replies* demonstrate certain common assumptions and inconsistencies. Language demands were frequently brought up within the context of the subject of English. The readiness with which difficulties associated with spelling, grammar and reading were identified did not extend to problems associated with language forms and usage. Indeed, at times a great deal of explaining and many examples were needed to show to the satisfaction of some teachers that context influences language use and thus the form of the language employed. There was a tendency among the teachers to think of their own classroom language as simple and clear, while at the same time being ignorant of its characteristic features. Most were unaware of the existence of different language varieties and had no knowledge of the extent to which they were represented in subject teaching or other school activities.

It would be a mistake to think these responses surprising or reprehensible. The vast majority of the populace would be

---

* By the end of the study well over a hundred teachers had been involved in the discussions.

less aware of language behaviour than the sample of teachers who have through their work become alerted to some aspects. Nor is this quite natural state of affairs likely to change significantly. Linguistics is a specialised discipline, and a relatively recent one at that, so its influence upon public awareness of the forms and functions of language is small. However, for teachers, a rudimentary understanding of relevant linguistic studies—i.e., those that have been applied in the field of education—could provide valuable and, indeed, crucial insights that cannot be obtained from the other fields of study that contribute to our understanding of language.

One linguistic notion that is highly applicable to the discussion of the language demands of subject learning is that of varieties of language distinguished according to use, or 'registers' as they are sometimes termed. In attempting to study this further, we can follow the suggestion Halliday (1964) made in respect of the study of institutional linguistics: that a useful starting-point is the notion of a language community as 'a group of speakers who regard themselves as using the same language'. This places the emphasis on the way in which language is used, a criterion which enables us to distinguish the different varieties within the language community.

A speaker of English will always use his language in a manner which is peculiar to him: thus, we can distinguish variety according to user. Slight local differences in patterns of intonation and pronunciation, etc., are referred to as 'accents', while peculiar personal use that shows considerable deviation from the standard form is referred to as a 'dialect'.

Varieties identified along this dimension are accepted phenomena of most complex language communities. They are likely to cause problems only if:

(*a*)   The particular variety is sufficiently deviant from the standard form that it cannot be considered to be the same language as that used by the others who constitute the vast majority of speakers in the language community, and (*b*)   the standard form is not freely available to dialect users and used by them in at least some part of their discourse or writing.

We also know that, in the sense that a speaker has a range of possibilities open to him which are subject to the constraints of the situation for which the language is required, it is *use* rather than user which in this case is the distinguishing feature. In other words, language varies with its function, differing with different situations in an attempt to meet the peculiar demands made upon it.

It is possible to study varieties of English—which are many, for we are dealing with a complex language community—by studying either the performer or the language itself. The latter method is the one that concerns us, and thus account is taken of the subject of discourse, different modes within writing and speech, and the relation between participants in any piece of language. There is no simple solution for this sort of study. Ure (1969), writing about the concern of descriptive linguistics to identify and describe registers, warns that:

> We cannot pick on a set of 'desirable circumstances', find out what sort of language goes with them, and then lay down that it shall be used on all occasions. This would be to deny the idea of 'appropriateness'. No one register can serve as an all-purpose model.

She goes on to say that it is obviously desirable that practical language uses should be understood by students and that the best way to produce an awareness of one form of language patterning is to compare it with another. The criterion is to be appropriacy and not which is 'better'.

The idea of appropriacy has been given prominence by McIntosh (1966). He says that a speaker wishing to say something to fit a given situation will need to select one utterance and therefore will be preoccupied with the suitability of the utterance for the context in which it is required. He considers the quality of appropriacy to be a necessary condition for the utterance to qualify as suitable. However, although this is the case, appropriacy is not the sole criterion on which the success of the utterance must be judged. What the speaker may decide is appropriate can be unsuccessful because it is not adequate. By adequate McIntosh means: 'the way in which a piece of linguistic activity "works" in specific connection with those aspects of a situation that are relevant to the achievement of some sort of objective'. With this definition it is possible for an utterance or, for that matter, a piece of writing to be appropriate but not adequate—i.e., it does not achieve its objective within the situation. On the other hand, as appropriacy is a necessary quality for success, what qualifies as adequate can be regarded as appropriate since the notion of adequacy subsumes the quality of appropriacy. Thus, a question to be asked when attempting a comparison of different registers is what are the distinctive qualities that make each utterance or text appropriate for the particular situation?

Before going on to discuss the place of register in schools it may be helpful to consider some general features of register contrast. One such example is formal and colloquial English which influences the vocabulary and, even more so, the idioms of a language. An obvious lexical difference is that large numbers of words are found only in very limited fields; but equally important in this respect, as Strevens (1966) points out, is the 'company that each keeps, in the co-occurrence of some words and the mutual exclusiveness of others'. As an example he notes that the register of astronomy contains words like 'star', 'planet', 'constellation', but that 'horoscope' does not occur. However, in the register of astrology, 'horoscope' does collocate with terms which are also found in astronomy.

Grammatical differences of register are not immediately as obvious as lexical ones, and require that the language be analysed thoroughly. Leech (1966), writing about the register of advertising, suggests four principles upon which register analysis is based:

1   Register distinctions are mostly relative not absolute.

2   People are often unaware of the register distinctions they operate.
3   The conventions of register are not invisible—register could be those conventions (rather than rules) which restrict linguistic behaviour according to use.
4   Differences of register are statistically measurable.

Leech provides a useful model for analysing and charting register distinctions which will be given later, as it was used by the present writer to analyse the language of the lessons obtained for the investigation of register use in the classroom, which will also be described.

We come now to the discussion of the contention made earlier that children encounter and have to come to terms with registers in school, including those with difficult linguistic features such as scientific English. In the opening chapters mention was made of the work of Taylor (1968), which provides strong evidence in support of the contention. Another study is that of Biddulph (1963), which was concerned with the features of chemistry, physics and biology texts, including a number of school texts. He came to the conclusion that his grammatical and lexical analysis of the texts identified a scientific register and certain sub-registers, each related to a specific science subject.

The description of a study of classroom language by Barnes (1969), which was given in the previous chapter, has already introduced evidence of the existence of register in classroom dialogue between teachers and pupils. Barnes does not offer information regarding the features of subject registers. In fact, he reserves his comments for what he calls the 'register of secondary education', describing it in these terms:

> The register referred to has much in common with the language of textbooks, of official publications, of almost any printed document that sets out to discuss a topic in an impersonal public way. . . . The register, being a spoken one, overlaps still more with the language of public debate and discussion in which the business of the community is carried on, in meetings and committees of greater or less formality.

The study carried out by the present writer was not so much concerned with learning more about this particular register as attempting to identify any existing subject registers and describe their characteristics. The language of biology teaching was selected for particular attention, but as the method adopted for the investigation of this part of the work was that of *register contrast* it was necessary to analyse the language of a selection of school subjects.

The questions that prompted the investigation have a direct bearing on the contention that children encounter and have to come to terms with different registers in school, and were as follows:

(*a*) Bearing in mind the importance of context with regard to the choice of appropriate language, what are the demands made upon the language of the child in the school in general and in the learning situations associated with the different subjects of the curriculum? The specific hypotheses* tested for these questions were:
1 There is no difference between the language a child encounters in school and his ordinary speech.
2 There is no significant difference in the demands made upon a child's language by the different subjects of the curriculum.

(*b*) Bearing in mind that it is possible to recognise different registers and to identify their linguistic features, can registers be identified in the school and to what extent do they relate to individual subjects? The specific hypotheses tested were:
3 That the linguistic features of the language used in the various subject lessons are not sufficiently differentiated as to suggest that they constitute different registers.

In designing the research it was necessary to consider what particular methods would be most effective for investigating

* For convenience in relation to statistical treatment, the hypotheses are in the null form.

the different hypotheses. Clearly, a descriptive and analytical design was indicated for the identification and comparison of specific registers. The need to categorise and count certain of the linguistic units contained in the different subject texts is met by the descriptive element. 'Analytical' refers to the fact that the study is set up to explore also the relationship between particular variables.

Within the design of any study, the experimenter is concerned with four types of variable. First, there is the dependent variable. This is the one with which the study primarily deals, in this case whether or not someone uses a register. The second type covers the independent variables whose effect upon the dependent variable the experimenter is trying to find. In this case they are factors like subject matter, teaching style, a child's conceptual level, etc. The third group contains the controlled variables. Here the experimenter tries to prevent factors other than the independent ones from influencing the dependent variable. This may be accomplished by controls which hold certain factors constant and by matching samples. In this study both methods were used, the former in connection with the collection, transcription and analysis of taped lessons, and the latter in connection with experimental and control groups from the pupil samples. The fourth group of variables comprises those uncontrolled factors which affect the experiment by chance. Such was the possibility that the presence of the tape-recorder caused some teachers unconsciously to change their normal language forms.

THE SAMPLES

For the hypotheses that have been discussed some seventy tapes were required from which the final selection was made. This is constituted as follows: biology—ten lessons, giving a total of around 20,000 words; English, mathematics, history, geography, foreign languages, physics, chemistry—five lessons in each, constituting some 10,000 words per subject.

For all the work, comprehensive schools and the primary schools in their catchment areas in five different regions of the country were used. This was to keep the type of school constant, while avoiding a local influence. Because the participation of teachers was essential to the success of the work, the presence in two suitable schools of a member of staff known to the present writer positively influenced the choice. However, a major influence on the success of this part of the work was the high level of co-operation obtained from staff in all the schools approached.

OBTAINING, TRANSCRIBING AND ANALYSING
TAPES OF LESSONS

Arrangements for visiting a school for a period of one week for the purpose of taping lessons were made in advance. On arrival, contact was made with the teachers who had indicated their willingness to participate in the investigation, so that arrangements for recording could be made. At times it was necessary to persuade more teachers to co-operate and to request specific subjects, age bands and ability groups so that for *each subject sample*:

1 The number of lessons taped was the same (except biology, where twice as many tapes were required).
2 Each lesson was taught by a different teacher.
3 The age bands 11-12 years, 13-14 years and 15-16 years were represented.
4 The ability groups below-average, average, above-average, and mixed ability were represented.

Teachers were assured that their names would not be connected with the tape in any way and that if after recording a lesson they wished to withhold the tape they were free to do so.* The instructions given to each teacher were:

1 Take a typical lesson containing some class dialogue.
2 Teach in your normal style, doing nothing out of the ordinary.
3 Keep a record of the number of different pupils involved in class dialogue.

* No teacher withheld a tape.

The tape-recorder was set up in a concealed position in the classroom and the microphone made as inconspicuous as possible. The tape-recorder was switched on immediately prior to the entry of the pupils into the room and switched off and removed after they had left. This procedure proved quite successful in preventing pupils from realising that the lesson was being recorded, for most teachers reported that the class was unaware of the presence of the recording equipment. In the relatively few cases where it was thought that pupils were aware that they were being recorded, after the initial reaction they appeared to forget this and respond normally. At the time of collection labels were attached to the tapes giving details of the region, subject, age band, ability and number of pupil responses.

The transcriptions were completed as follows:

1   All tapes were transcribed on the first play.
2   All tapes were given a second play, concentrating on filling the gaps in the first transcription.
3   All tapes were given a third play to check the transcription for small errors.
4   Two further attempts were made to improve the transcription of poorer-quality recordings. Any gaps still remaining were shown on the transcriptions as such.

Eventually, some forty-five technically acceptable tapes were obtained ready for analysis.

As the amount of pupil language in a lesson is largely controlled by the teacher, and at secondary level a common method of affording pupils opportunities to respond is through questioning, the analytical model used by Barnes (1969) in his study (as mentioned in the previous chapter) was employed. With it, it was hoped to identify the different functions for which pupils had to find the language and to demonstrate the presence or absence of *patterns* of functional demands peculiar to specific subjects. It was also expected that the model would show the degree of pupil participation and the existence of specialised or complex language sufficiently different from ordinary speech as to present problems for some pupils.

The model proved to have certain limitations that caused problems similar to those identified by Barnes (1969) when using it to analyse his sample of lessons. These are listed below:

1 The categories were not always sufficiently sensitive to make possible accurate classification.
2 It was necessary to interpret the kind of answer required by a teacher in assigning questions to categories: e.g., a question could appear to be seeking information when in reality the teacher was concerned with obtaining a name.
3 It was not possible always to know with certainty if the reasoning activity requested of a pupil was 'new' or concerned with summing up required knowledge from memory. Thus, unless the lesson was obviously a revision of work, it was difficult to decide if the reasoning was recalled or not recalled.
4 Categorising open questions proved to be difficult. Questions which on the surface appeared to be open frequently had a very limited number of correct or acceptable answers. It was decided that freedom of choice (where necessary within the bounds of reason) should be an essential element in criteria for deciding openness. Thus questions which could be answered only by the selection of one of a very limited number of correct responses were categorised as closed.

The results related to the first hypothesis (that there is no difference between the language a child encounters in school and his ordinary speech) suggest that in school pupils encounter language forms which *are* different from their ordinary speech. Characteristically such language shows increased formality of style, makes use of a specialised vocabulary and contains certain repetitive patterns of syntactic structure which are often more complex than would occur in the language normally employed by the pupil. In some cases the language is peculiar to the subject and appears to have a useful function in that it carries concepts and meanings that cannot be readily expressed in other forms.

However, not all the complex language present had this kind of function; some appeared to be related to the activity of instructing, its style being that of what Barnes (1969) calls the 'language of secondary education'.

Differences can be detected among the subjects represented in the sample in respect of the frequency with which the characteristics mentioned above make their appearance (see Table 1). Specialised language forms appear more frequently in science subjects than in arts subjects, while increased formality and language outside the pupil's range are more evenly distributed throughout the subjects. In this respect biology clusters with physics, mathematics and chemistry, although the features are more strongly represented in physics and chemistry.

A feature worthy of note was that formal or specialised language from the teacher tended to elicit a similar style of language from the pupils responding. A physics lesson with 12-year-old pupils of average and slightly above average ability in a secondary modern school provides numerous examples of this, a sample of which is given below:

'that they knew all about matter'
'the very smallest particle of matter'
'liquid conductors of electricity'
'it had to do with passing an electric current through a gas'
'gases at very low pressures, sir'
'Marie Curie died from the effects of radiation'

We can perhaps see more clearly how this is happening if we look at yet another response from the same lesson and include the teacher's question and comment.

Teacher: It was discovered that there were rays, that rays were found to respond to magnets and J. J. Thompson—I think you have studied Thompson, have you not?—was responsible for discovering what?

Pupil: That rays had weight, sir.

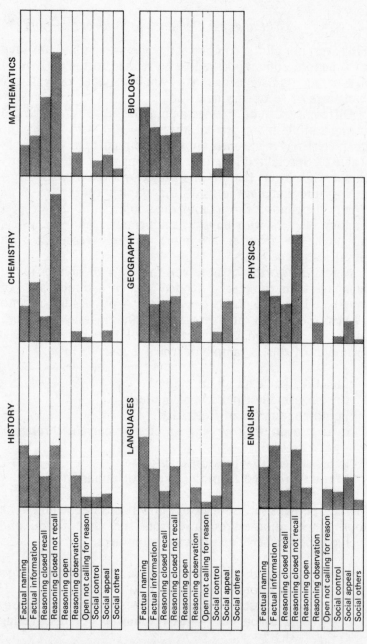

Table 1 *Distribution of Individual Categories of Question as a Proportion of all Questions Asked within the Lessons of Each Subject Sample*

Teacher: Yes, to use an ordinary term, 'weight'; but technically the term is 'mass'....

This teacher signals his language expectations to his pupils, and it is likely that the pupils' responses combine a conscious effort to find 'acceptable' scientific terms and an unconscious use of the forms employed by the teacher.

On the occasions that teacher and pupils are engaged in class dialogue the proportion of the time taken up by the total pupil talk is very small. Maths and English had the best record, approaching a fifty-fifty distribution. Frequently pupil talk occupied less than 15 per cent of the time. In all lessons the utterances tended to be short; between one and eight words was common, and this contrasts markedly with the length of utterances obtained from group discussions involving a small number of pupils. There are numerous examples of lengthy teacher utterances that finish up with a question requiring one word to fill the slot:

Teacher: Just imagine filling up a truck full of coal and taking it to the edge and giving it a push. It would go down of its own accord, wouldn't it? Of course they didn't just do that. They had lines for it...tracks, and they used the full trucks going down to pull up the...?
Pupil: Empties.
Teacher: Empties, right...

Bearing in mind this tendency, and the fact that most classes contained around thirty pupils, clearly 'class dialogue' does not give individual pupils much opportunity for exploring and expressing ideas.

To understand more about the nature of the differences among subjects it is necessary to concentrate on the results of the analysis used in the second hypothesis—that there is no significant difference in the demands made upon a child's language by the different subjects of the curriculum. Inspection of the subject histograms indicates that distinctions do exist among subjects, one being the proportion of factual to reasoning questions within a subject. For example, mathematics makes nearly twice the reasoning demand of any of the arts subjects. Physics and chemistry also show considerably higher proportions of reasoning questions than the remaining subjects. In the same category biology is slightly ahead of the arts subjects, its reasoning score being identical with its factual score. This factual score is second highest to geography and puts biology further ahead of the remaining arts subjects in the category than these same arts subjects are ahead of physics and chemistry.

To obtain finer distinctions with regard to the kinds of factual and reasoning questions, it is necessary to look at the individual categories. A notable point is that half the subjects (geography, languages, biology, history) have larger proportions of factual-naming questions than factual information. This trend is particularly noticeable in geography. The four individual reasoning categories show a less even distribution among each other than exists among the subjects of which they are constituted. The most strongly represented group is 'reasoning closed not recalled', but in considering this result the limitations of the analytical model should be borne in mind. It is highly likely that the 'not recalled' category contains questions in which earlier work *was* being recalled, although this could not be identified from the context of the lesson.

Observation of the subjects which constitute the categories shows an equal distribution of arts and science subjects (physics, biology, geography, chemistry and history) clustering at the middle of the 'reasoning recalled' category. In the 'reasoning not recalled' category biology, geography and history are joined by English at the middle range, while physics and chemistry with mathematics each shows at least twice the proportion of questions as any of the other subjects.

The English lessons contained only a small number of open questions, but this still put them well ahead of any other subject. While it is true that the criteria for identifying openness did not allow questions with a very limited choice of answers, a greater preponderance of open-reasoning questions was expected in English and history and to a lesser degree in geography and languages. The lack of open reasoning in mathematics, physics, chemistry and to a lesser degree biology was not so surprising. At the conceptual level of the pupils represented in the samples, much of the lesson time is taken up with the presentation of large numbers of factual concepts and the organisation of practical work, both activities which call for a great deal of explanation. Science teachers tend to check the effectiveness of their explanations through the use of questions which have a very limited (if any) choice of correct answers.

The last group of reasoning questions, those concerned with observation, with two exceptions show a fairly even distribution among the subjects. Biology is ahead of the other subjects, but not as far as could have been expected in view of its intrinsic nature. Indeed, careful observation is such an essential part of the subject's method of inquiry that this category seems under-represented in the lessons recorded for the study. The two exceptions are also noteworthy. The low score in chemistry is surprising if teachers are making use of experimental methods in their lessons, while English is not represented at all in this category. One possible explanation for the latter is that not one of the taped lessons was based on a set book. Thus, textual observations were not required. In one lesson pupils were discussing a poem. They were asked to express opinions about the meaning, but during this exercise were not directed to an examination of the relevant sections of the text.

The appearance of social questions in subjects appears random. As a phenomenon it seems to be associated more with teacher style than with the subject being taught. Social appeal is more strongly represented than social control, and most likely because there is a conscious or unconscious desire on the part of teachers to avoid direct confrontation.

THE LINGUISTIC FEATURES OF SUBJECT LANGUAGE

To obtain more precise information about the linguistic features of the language used between teacher and pupil within subject disciplines, and to test the third hypothesis (that the linguistic features of the language used in the various subject lessons are not sufficiently differentiated as to suggest that they constitute different registers), a more precise analysis of the transcripts was necessary. The analytical model used is based on that of Leech (1966) referred to earlier. The categories retained were those thought to be suitable for charting the characteristics of the rather specialised kind of dialogue between teacher and pupils in the lesson samples obtained. The features selected for analysis represent various dimensions organised as outlined below:

A. *Style of Discourse*
Relation between participants—in this case between teacher and pupil—is considered under the heading of 'style of discourse' using four sets of polarities of style:

1 COLLOQUIAL-FORMAL
   'Colloquial' is associated with a private style; i.e., it is used between participants who know one another, in informal situations. Indicators in the texts of this style are: the presence of idioms, slang, phrasal verbs, contractions and imperatives.
   'Formal' is associated with a public style. Indicators in the texts of this style are: the absence of colloquial features, the presence of unspecified origins and destinations of the communication and the extent to which individual source and address are irrelevant to the message.
Not all the features used as indicators of colloquial and formal styles are susceptible of clear-cut definition. Listed below are those features for which it is thought necessary to give examples and additional information.
   Idioms: These are of the sort that would be found in books of idiomatic phrases prepared for students studying English as a second language—e.g., 'Let's look at the ins and outs', 'they found themselves out of pocket', 'it goes without saying'.
   Contractions: e.g., 'don't', 'gonna', 'we've'.

Imperatives: In addition to the obvious use of the imperative there are frequent instances of the teacher avoiding the imperative form while at the same time requiring pupils to perform a particular action—e.g., 'let's all look at the results', 'will you hurry up and complete the experiments?' Examples of this sort have been counted as imperatives.

Phrasal verbs: These consist of a verb (often of high frequency and unspecific meaning) and a particle—e.g., 'find out', 'look at', 'get on' (with work). They are used in place of a single verb of more specific meaning.

Unspecified origins: Where at the initiating end of a linguistic message there is a degree of anonymity of authorship—e.g., 'To eat the wrong kind of food may be as bad for you as not eating at all.' 'South Wales is divided up into three or four counties, and over to the west you can see Pembroke.'

Unspecified destinations: Where at the receiving end of a linguistic message there is a degree of anonymity of addressee—e.g., 'I want to know the name biologists give to an animal which has both male and female reproductive organs on the same organism.' 'Suppose I have oil or grease on my hands; what would happen upon washing in soapy water?' 'I have three pictures which depict the sort of places in which the Anglo-Saxons settled.'

Individual source and address irrelevant to the message: Where at the initiating and receiving end of a linguistic message neither origin nor destination is specifiable—e.g., 'It has been seen that the elements sulphur and carbon are similar in several respects.' 'With the fall of Rome in the West, civilisation and learning shifted from Europe into the Near East.'

2 CASUAL-CEREMONIAL

'Casual' is bound to the same set of linguistic features as 'colloquial', but it is not identifiable with it in terms of all its characteristics. Indicators in the texts of this style are: the presence of intimate forms of address, use of ordinary conversational language by teachers and pupils.

'Ceremonial' is bound to the linguistic features of 'formal' after the manner described in the 'casual'-'colloquial' relationship. Indicators in the texts of this style are: use of polite forms of address, changes in the language of ordinary conversation towards the careful, deferential and formal, replacement of demands by requests.

3 PERSONAL-IMPERSONAL

'Personal' shares many of the linguistic features of 'colloquial' and 'casual' but, again, it is not identifiable with either in terms of its characteristics. Indicators in the texts of this style are: free use of first- and second-person reference, use of third person for reference to named individuals, use of imperatives, questions and exclamations which involve the first and second person without direct reference.

Impersonality is unlikely to occur in private discourse. In public discourse it is associated with anonymity of participants and therefore with the upper end of the formality scale. Indicators in the texts of this style are: absence of first- and second-person pronouns, presence of third-person forms to evade reference to author and addressee, passive voice, non-finite verb forms.

4 SIMPLE-COMPLEX

'Complexity' can be given a more precise linguistic meaning by equating it with the number of elements of structure per grammatical unit. Thus, indicators in the texts of a complex style are: the number of words per sentence, the number of clauses per sentence, the number of main (independent) clauses to subordinate (dependent) clauses per sentence.

B. *Mode of Discourse*

The manner in which language varies according to medium will be investigated by comparing the teacher's spoken transmission of the subject matter of a lesson with the written transmission of the subject matter of the same topic in a relevant textbook. Indicators in the paired texts of distinctions between the media are: a tendency for the increased appearance in the written text of certain linguistic features present in the spoken text; a tendency for the decreased appearance in the written texts of certain other linguistic features present in the spoken text; the absence in either text of linguistic features present in the other.

C. *Role of Discourse*
Two phenomena are considered under this head:

1 ROLE SPECIALISATION

Roles divide broadly into two types: 'conservative' and 'liberal'. 'Conservative' refers to roles in which all pressure is towards conformity to accepted linguistic conventions. Indicators in the texts of this type are: presence of a special vocabulary, repeated appearance of particular language structures, a tendency for the linguistic features of style to be interrelated—'e.g. 'formal', 'impersonal' and 'complex'. 'Liberal' refers to roles in which the main tendency is towards originality and inventiveness of language. Indicators in the texts of this type are: unusual use of words or groups of words, presence of varied language structures, absence of linguistic specialisation.

2 ROLE BORROWING

This refers to the use in one role of the linguistic features appropriate to another. The indicator in the texts of this phenomenon is: the appearance of linguistic features which are different from those which constitute the major part of the text.

The model obviously has limitations. In the first place, to describe linguistic features it is necessary to use specialised language so as to avoid inaccuracy and ambiguity. This is not an easy task, for over the past thirty years or so grammatical description has been at the centre of much argument among grammarians. In an effort to avoid being drawn into these controversies the terminology characteristic of so-called 'traditional' grammar is used. This terminology may not be the one most acceptable to modern linguists, but it has the advantage of being that with which many people are most familiar. It is also true that the chosen indicators of a particular style constitute only a limited selection of the linguistic features which could have been used and that the linguistic features selected as indicators of a particular style or role are those which were thought to be the most obvious from the standpoint of non-specialist teachers. Thus, the analysis is not aiming to achieve a high degree of sensitivity.

Each indicator of a particular feature relating to one or other of the dimensions of discourse—i.e., style, mode and role—was identified on the transcripts, and totals obtained for individual subject samples. It was then possible to see the characteristics of one subject in relation to any other.

On the dimension of style of discourse, using the features selected as indicators, the subjects tended to cluster into arts and science groupings. The science group was constituted of mathematics, physics, chemistry and biology scores, and the arts group of English, geography, languages and history scores.

The arts group shows a more colloquial style than the science group, and the science group a significantly more formal style than the arts group. This is repeated for the features indicating respectively the colloquial-formal and personal-impersonal polarities of style. The casual-ceremonial features showed a random distribution among the subjects with one exception—namely, English—which had more casual and fewer ceremonial features than any other subject.

On the polarities of style, therefore, the language of the arts subjects is to some extent more colloquial and personal than that of the sciences, though the *degree* varies from one indicator to another. The features indicating a colloquial style exemplify this. One possible explanation is that in classroom language some features are less reliable indicators of a particular style than others. For example, the imperative used for recipe in science lessons produces language structures which tend towards the formal rather than towards the colloquial—for example, 'Add the solution in test tube A to the suspension in the flask and shake up.' There was a relatively small representation of idioms even in those subjects which could have been expected to have a high representation. Contractions, on the other hand, were in such common use that they made their appearance in pieces of language of otherwise formal style.

The language of science subjects, though appearing to be more complex, did not show up as clearly so on the features chosen as indicators. It is likely that a different method of indicating complexity could have been employed which would have discriminated more clearly between the two groups. For example, the use of recursive structure in definition may be a better indicator of complexity than sentence length. Such structures are very commonly found in science subjects.

B. MODE OF DISCOURSE

In the comparison of the spoken transmission of the subject matter of each lesson with the written transmission of the subject matter of the same topic in a relevant class textbook, English afforded some problems. Two of the lessons were discussions without reference to any texts, two could be described as literature (although the work was not related to a set book), and the remaining one was concerned with the use of language in the writing of a specific letter. The situation appeared to demand the examination of a range of books (novels, anthologies of verse, prose extracts, language texts) in use by the class and considered by the present writer to be representative of the content of the recorded lessons.

The results of the comparison for the eight subjects represented by the lesson samples are as follows:

1 A tendency for the increased appearance in the written transmission of the formal, impersonal and complex features present in the spoken text. One geography written text proved an exception; this was from an activity book, the style of which showed no noticeable increase in the appearance of the above features.

2 A tendency for the reduced appearance in the written transmission of the colloquial, personal and simple

features present in the spoken transmission. Certain English written texts proved to be exceptions. In these there was a tendency for the increased appearance of idioms, third-person reference to named individuals and relatively short sentences. These features are respectively indicators of colloquial, personal and simple styles.

Most written texts in all subjects show increased formality, a characteristic common to this mode of transmission when compared with spoken English. However, a notable feature is that much of the vocabulary constituting the written texts of physics, chemistry and biology *is* present in the spoken texts of those subjects. The proportion undergoes a progressive reduction through geography, mathematics, history and language until in the case of English a relatively small proportion of it is present in the rather limited vocabulary of the spoken texts. Thus, although features indicating certain trends relating to medium are common to all subjects, differences of degree exist.

While it was not intended that lexical features should be accounted indicators of difference in style between written and spoken transmission, these were sufficiently obvious in the English text to be noteworthy. Nearly half the vocabulary encountered in the range of written texts was absent from the range of spoken texts, while the reverse was not true. In two written texts unusual word collocations were present—for example, 'The wakes of gunboats sew the green dark with speed'; 'the air that shudders black with snow'. Features of this kind did not, in fact, appear in any spoken language, and the range of vocabulary used was narrower than in any other subject. One possible explanation for this is that all but one of the lessons involved class discussion around a specific topic, an activity generally directed by the teacher through questioning. However, as was also noted by Barnes (1976), such questioning does not necessarily call out a high degree of explicitness. A low degree may occur because when responding to questions pupils sense that their teachers know the answer already. Thus, it is not necessary to offer a full explanation but only to convince them that you have 'got it right'. Many pupils seem to be so much in the habit of responding in this way that they will not explore ideas or venture opinions even when invited to do so by the teacher. It may be also that they are loath to expose tentative ideas before a group the size of a typical school class which may or may not react favourably to them.

C. ROLE OF DISCOURSE

1 ROLE SPECIALISATION

It was intended that both 'conservative' and 'liberal' types of role specialisation would be considered, but the analysis disclosed few positive indicators of a liberal role in any texts. It was decided, therefore, to note indicators of the conservative type (which refers to roles in which all pressure is towards conformity to accepted linguistic conventions) and identify the degree of role conservatism peculiar to each subject.

Indicators of a conservative role

(a) *Special vocabulary*

In arriving at the number of technical terms present in the samples, the first appearance of a term in any lesson was counted. After the first appearance of a term in a lesson, subsequent appearances in the same lesson were not counted. The same procedure was used for counting terms which, though not technical, regularly appear either in the company of technical terms or in language forms associated with the subject matter—for example, in biology 'uptake' (of), 'articulate' (with) are two such cases.

The actual number of such terms counted in the five lessons constituting each subject sample is given in Table 2. From it we can see that special and technical terms are in common use in all subjects and that the scores in the science group could be used to support the contention that in these subjects pupils are overburdened with technical vocabulary.

Table 2

	Feature	
Subject	Technical term	Special non-technical term
Mathematics	111	57
Physics	249	45
Chemistry	223	32
Geography	110	21
English	34	42
History	79	48
Languages	52	49
Biology	225	63

(b) *Repeated appearance of particular language structures*

The above feature was found to be common to all texts analysed. The appearance and re-appearance of a structure tended to coincide with a particular function being performed by the language—for example, description, explanation, etc. In turn, the number and variety of functions which the language was expected to perform were determined by the nature of the subject.

(c) *A tendency for the linguistic features of style to be interrelated*

Examination of the results shows that the formal, impersonal and complex features are interrelated and that mathematics, physics, chemistry and biology use this style more often than the other subjects in the sample. Similarly the colloquial, personal and simple features are interrelated and appear more frequently in English, languages and history than in the other subjects in the sample.

The results associated with role of discourse indicate two varieties of role specialisation, both of the conservative type. English, history, geography and languages share colloquial, personal, relatively less complex stylistic features and low scores for technical and special terms. Mathematics, physics, chemistry and biology share formal, impersonal, relatively more complex stylistic features and high scores for technical and special terms. The occurrence of particular language structures is marked enough in the science subjects to suggest that the register of scientific English exerts a powerful influence on the language of science teachers in spite of their attempts to adapt their language to the needs of the pupils. Use of the register is particularly noticeable when material is being exposed, terms defined and information recorded.

2   ROLE BORROWING

The use in one role of the linguistic features of another was encountered in all lessons. However, although role borrowing occurred in all subjects, it is more marked in physics, chemistry and biology, though history and geography teachers also made considerable use of this device. In science it occurs most frequently when a teacher's first priority is to promote understanding in the pupil. A common technique employed is the use of analogy, for which on most occasions a colloquial, simple, often personal style is used which is much closer to the pupils' ordinary speech. The age and ability of the class influences the amount of role borrowing employed, as does the conceptual level of the material being taught. There is a steady increase in the use of the register of scientific English and a decrease in the phenomenon of role borrowing as pupils move up the school and as their knowledge and understanding of the concepts of the subjects expand and deepen.

It would seem, on the face of the evidence available, that differences among subjects relating to role specialisation are associated with at least two different forms of a conservative role. That inventive language appears to be in short supply in the spoken medium is to be expected when we look at the subject matter of the lessons and the language functions it calls forth. We would perhaps have expected English to have compensated for this deficiency more than was the case, but it may be that writing is the preferred medium for activities of this nature.

Taking together the results associated with style, mode and role of discourse, there appears to be ground for asserting that within schools language varieties exist which can be thought of as rudimentary registers* that become increasingly differentiated and in evidence with the pupil's progress through the school. The degree to which a particular variety becomes more or less developed is dependent also upon the level of the course. When teaching 'O' and 'A' level courses teachers tend to employ language that is closer to the subject norm depicted in supporting texts than they do when teaching CSE or remedial courses.

What Barnes (1969) calls the 'language of secondary education' is also subject to the influences described above. Indeed, it could be hypothesised that once a teacher feels the need to fall back upon subject language to express his meanings (which in most subjects causes him to use a more formal, impersonal and complex style than that of everyday speech) he becomes set in the style and continues to use it where 'ordinary' language would be entirely adequate and have the advantage of being more readily understood by the pupils. Nor can we ignore the possibility that, in relation to the dimension Leech (1966) identifies as role of discourse, the teacher is under unconscious pressure to conform to accepted linguistic conventions. The conventions may be imposed by the subject—i.e., a teacher of science may feel under pressure to conform to the accepted linguistic conventions of scientific English. On the other hand, the pressure may come from an individual's own concept of the role of a teacher—for example, the accepted linguistic conventions associated with the role of transmitting a body of knowledge.

At some point, as the analysis of linguistic features neared completion, it became apparent that the model's three dimensions of style, mode and role did not fully account for the significant variations within the language of the subject

---

*   To use Halliday's term for language variety.

lessons. The patterns and clusters of interrelated features tended to be directly associated with specific functions such as explaining, describing, hypothesising, reporting and recording, etc. This functional dimension appears at times to be operating with, and at other times cutting across, the dimensions of style, mode and role. Each function tends to produce a corresponding language structure. Tentative language (e.g., 'would' and 'could' sequences) is associated with hypothesising; complex recursive structures with defining. Thus, the degree to which each particular function is represented in the subject texts can be included usefully in the criteria for distinguishing the registers of subjects which share a number of linguistic features. For example, in the biology lessons as many words are used for describing and defining as for all four other functions. Chemistry, on the other hand, is the most strongly represented of the sciences in the category of explanation. This is the category which showed the greatest use of colloquial, personal and simple styles of language, often through the agency of role borrowing. The experimental nature of chemistry is reflected in the comparatively high incidence of hypothesis, report/record and recipe.

It is also clear that 'function' exercises a similar influence on the arts subjects. For example, the language used in geography teaching appears to change with the tendency for this subject to become increasingly concerned with quantifying rather than describing—a tendency which brings it closer to the register of science teaching. Similarly, history shows a progression from a concern with imparting information to a concern with the interpretation and evaluation of evidence, the tentative and hypothetical nature of this activity being reflected in the style of the language.

English enjoys a unique position among the subjects included in the study. As the results show, it often produced more 'homely' language than other subjects, largely because of the current pre-occupation with discussion of topical and social issues. However, this should not be allowed to obscure the fact that it is a subject that incorporates a wide range of language because of its concern with language as language and also with literature of various kinds. One point of difference concerns the latter in that a literary style employs a 'free' imaginative use of English. The characteristics of this style are often the opposite of those exhibited in scientific English on certain dimensions, but they nevertheless present pupils with their own peculiar difficulties. Indeed, the function of deliberate experimentation with language is not characteristic of most school subjects but is highly appropriate in the context of English teaching. Thus, one would expect the function to be a major concern of teachers of English. It is not possible in the functional categories represented in the total sample to take account of the overcomplication of language present in a great many of the lessons. Such language is neither ordinary and familiar nor an essential part of the register of the subject fulfilling a special role. Its lack of simplicity and directness causes difficulties associated with its inability to carry communications in a way that is readily understood by the pupil. It also fails to afford an acceptable model for use in the acquisition and development of the *necessary* specialised language of the subject.

The implications for teachers, and for those who advocate language policies in schools, of some of the points raised in the discussion of results will be considered later in relation to Fishman's concept of 'repertoire range' and the Bullock Report's (1974) reference to the need for 'a language for life'. However, before proceeding with this it is necessary to look at the crucial relationship between the notional and verbal aspects of concepts and the role of register in the development of subject concepts.

Chapter 5

Specialised Language and Concept Development

The current upsurge of interest in language and its functions has produced a climate in which a proposition that stresses the centrality of language in concept formation is likely to find unqualified acceptance. Such a high degree of agreement looks encouraging for the future promotion of enlightened methods and techniques which have as their objective the expansion of the conceptual function of language. But is such optimism justified? Language, specifically its role in learning in school, is now a fashionable topic. In common with the numerous other fashionable topics that have gone before, it has generated its own 'slogans' and 'in' expressions, the ready acceptance and use of which tend to prevent questioning of the sort that reveals the woolly, the ill-informed and the blinkered. Thus, the differences that may and almost certainly do exist among individuals with regard to their knowledge and understanding of the subject do not come to light. For example, how varied are individual notions of the *extent* to which language functions in conceptual development and of the *nature* of this function?

Any attempt to answer the question must take account of the processes involved in language acquisition and concept formation. To do so it is not possible to remain solely in the field of language or, for that matter, psychology, which is another field involved. As it is an interfunctional relationship that we have to try to understand, it is unlikely that this will be gained by separating language and thought for the purpose of analysis. Something like Vygotsky's notion (1962) of a verbal unit is required—i.e., his 'word-meaning', which contains the elements of thought and speech and avoids the problem of deciding the boundaries of each in relation to the other.

The exact relationship between thought and speech in the genesis of language and formation of concepts is still a vexed subject, and the agreement which characterises more general statements such as the one made earlier about the centrality of language in concept formation is lacking here. Much of the fruitful work in this field has been done respectively by Vygotsky and Bruner, but in their conclusions some points of disagreement are to be found. This appears less surprising once the complexity of the relationship is appreciated, and it reinforces the contention that to study language in this context it is necessary to come to terms with the psychological aspects of the problem as well as the linguistic.

To meet this need a summary follows of some major theories and useful observations from studies that have shed light on the role of language in concept formation and higher-order thinking. It is necessarily brief, and so condensed, but nonetheless takes account of a range of views about the nature of the relationship in question and the factors that are influential in the developmental sequences of language from birth through early childhood and the period of spontaneous learning, and on to the stage of formal learning. As far as is possible, particular functions of language at specific stages of development will be emphasised, including those considered to be very relevant to school learning.

Vygotsky's experimental studies (1962) led him to believe that ontogenetically speech and thought develop from different roots, with speech having a pre-intellectual stage and thought a pre-linguistic stage. The two develop independently and along separate lines up to a certain point in time when the lines converge and thought becomes verbal and speech rational. The nature of the development is at first biological, but since verbal thought is determined by cultural processes it changes to the socio-historical quite early on and this remains the dominant influence as the child learns socially reinforced names for his own internal representation of experience.

Vygotsky's explanations have found considerable support, but this has not prevented alternative theories being offered, most of which accept some of Vygotsky's conclusions while taking issue with others. One example is Bruner (1966), who rejects Vygotsky's notion of different ontogenetîc roots, affirming that language comes from the same basic root as that of symbolically organised experience. He sees this activity as something basic and primitive that is realised most fully in language and finally in the organisation of experience through concept formation. He agrees with Vygotsky that, early on, the nature of the development is increasingly social, noting that given cultural support a child in an advanced society becomes operational*—i.e., able to think symbolically—between the age of 5 and 7. Bruner sees the nature of an individual's development as involving the interrelation of the ways of acting, imagining and symbolising that are in existence in that individual's culture. The development of these powers will depend upon:

(*a*) the supply of amplifiers—i.e., images, skills, concepts, etc., that a culture contains;

(*b*) the nature of the life led by the individual; and

(*c*) the extent to which he is incited to explore the sources of concordance or discordance of his mode of knowing. He makes a further point that the pressures to be found in technological societies demand confirmation between the three modes of knowing (i.e., acting, imagining and symbolising) and thus produce a need for correspondence between what we do, say and perceive. It is this correspondence which is involved in much school learning and other abstract pursuits.

Although the first concepts that arise do so unreflectively, in the sense that the semantic elements are not brought explicitly into the consciousness of the child, they nevertheless stimulate language in categories of the sort that Halliday

---

* This term, when used in the context of educational psychology, is normally associated with Jean Piaget's theory of intellectual development. This suggests that development occurs in identifiable stages, the child becoming capable of using increasingly complex forms of logical operation. He is referred to as becoming operational when he enters the stage at which he is able to represent phenomena symbolically.

(1969) calls 'instrumental', 'interactional' and 'personal' in his functional models of language. The growing awareness of the environment promotes the child's verbal knowledge by throwing up a rich variety of concepts that must be symbolised in words. At this stage the formation of concepts that have arisen as the result of reflective reconstruction will have begun. Once the child is consciously forming in the mind elements of new concepts, he stimulates language use in dimensions such as naming, ideational fluency and, in making his own propositions, fluency of expression.

Vygotsky (1962) calls these first unreflective concepts 'spontaneous' concepts, distinguishing between them and non-spontaneous (or scientific) concepts. The latter kind are those he considers likely to start life as verbal definitions. This being the case, the development of a spontaneous concept must have reached a certain stage for the child to be able to 'absorb' a related non-spontaneous one. The reason he offers is that the upward progression of the spontaneous concept clears the way for the non-spontaneous concept to work its way into the child's understanding—giving substance to the verbal definition. Thus, everyday concepts supply the structure for the genesis of non-spontaneous concepts, which in turn assist in the development of the child's spontaneous concepts towards increasingly deliberate use and, in doing so, demonstrate that inner ties exist between them. One example of this is that from their inception non-spontaneous concepts carry within them relationships of generality, the beginnings of a system. The discipline of this process influences the child's spontaneous concepts and helps organise them into a system. A similar tie exists between the thought and the word which identify with a particular concept. Vygotsky (1962) calls it a complex relationship in which the meaning of the word is a generalisation or a concept involving an act of thought. Thus, he regards word-*meaning* as a phenomenon of thinking, of dynamic formations which evolve and change as the child develops. Changes also occur in the relationship of thought to word. Words are not merely used to express thoughts; they are the means whereby thought comes into existence—

connecting one thing with another, so establishing relationships. Without words it would not be possible to envisage or indicate to someone else the limits of a concept—i.e., where it starts and finishes.

Roger Brown (1956) considers that concepts cannot be said to have been attained until the individual is able to recognise new instances of the concept without having to undergo further training. Similarly, a word can be considered fully understood when an individual can use it correctly in relation to entities that he has not heard labelled. He affirms that one cannot speak a language until the governing non-linguistic concepts are formed, but that this is not indicative of anything like a fixed relationship between names and the concepts they represent. In general, names indicate equivalence and, equally important, non-equivalence.

Carroll (1964) points out that there are different levels of difficulty involved in the attainment of concepts. Some concepts, such as certain scientific ones, require the attainment of pre-requisite concepts. He suggests that school learning involves concepts of intermediate difficulty which are usually acquired through the study of *verbal* formulations and the practice of recognition of instances and non-instances. He thinks that in teaching concepts verbal formulation is of great value, especially when followed by examples of positive and negative instances. The experiments of Spiker, Gerjuoy and Shepherd (1956) are referred to by him in support of his contention that, when in the course of normal day-to-day development a child learns a concept verbally, he tends to perform more successfully when faced with a problem in which the concept is critical, though not explicitly so.

Carroll warns that labels are useful only if they refer to a well-learned class. The value to the individual of having to use words in accordance with his speech community is that he must of necessity identify the corresponding stimuli. In this way language makes the differences between stimuli more noticeable than otherwise they would be. This development of verbal mediators has another striking effect—namely, it helps the individual to state and test hypotheses and appears to be highly correlated with mental development as measured by intelligence tests.

It would appear that conceptual language is very much the key to an individual's ability to make sense of his immediate environment and, indeed, through specific learning, such as that going on in school, to promote understanding and knowledge of things which would be unlikely to arise spontaneously in his ordinary everyday life. Unfortunately, though not unexpectedly in view of the complexity of the processes involved in concept formation, various difficulties may arise that exert their peculiar influence upon the conceptual development of the child. Our discussion of these will concentrate upon the difficulties associated with the verbal aspect of school subjects, for most contain a great deal of conceptual material and are very dependent upon language to carry their notional aspects in a way that is meaningful to the receiver. Adequate language, therefore, in this context is language that successfully takes account of pressures from two distinct sources, which are the subject and the receiver.

Ideally, it would be possible to make the assumption that the language 'capable' of adequately carrying a subject's concepts—i.e., carrying them accurately, fully, unambiguously and reasonably concisely—is also that which is understood readily by receiver, in this case a child. Furthermore, it could be argued that, where this assumption cannot be made, the concept should be regarded as too advanced for the developmental stage reached by the receiver. In reality, because the receivers that concern us are children, their initial understanding of non-spontaneous subject concepts is likely to be shallow, imperfect and lacking precision. There is nothing unexpected in this, for most concepts, even spontaneous ones, take time to mature, and many continue to grow with knowledge and experience throughout our lives. However, this fact must not be allowed to obscure the very real possibility that the notional aspects can be carried in the language in a way that satisfies the demands created by the nature of the subject but proves so unintelligible to the receiver that he fails to make contact with the notion or notions embodied in the concept.

When this happens with some regularity the child cannot make substantial gains in his understanding of the subjects' concepts, their nature, purpose or position in relation to each other. Nor can we allow ourselves the comfort of believing that this situation is rare, for in those subjects which have special vocabularies pupils are given the words early on to be gradually filled with experience, and the great danger of this is that a teacher may not realise that pupils may know many of the words he uses but do not share his meanings. Indeed, the erroneous carrying-over of personal meanings of words that have one specific meaning in the context of the particular subject is yet another very common phenomenon, and another associated difficulty is caused by teachers who introduce new notions using new words without giving explanations or precise definitions of the words. This leads to contextual ambiguity and prevents the growth of the concept by the normal process of it becoming more precise and relevant.

The use of technical terms can afford special difficulties in some subjects. Generally, a technical term represents a scientific concept. Children become familiar with non-scientific concepts first, and this can interfere with the acquisition of a scientific concept because the everyday meaning is at odds with the related scientific one.

Once subjects are concerned with the level of secondary concepts, they rely increasingly upon language. Definitions are employed with greater frequency which, although of little use in conveying a new concept, are able to convey concepts of the same or a lower order. Attempts by teachers to use definitions in the presentation of new notions can only cause difficulty for pupils since the main function of a definition is to set limits, a sort of tying-up of ends that cannot take place until after the concept has been formed.

The mention of conceptual levels reminds us that, in structuring learning material, assumptions are made in respect of some concepts being more readily acquired than others and, indeed, that the more complex concepts may demand the ability to identify several pre-requisite concepts in their proper sequence. By and large, it is the difficulty of the notional aspect of the concept that has served as the criterion rather than the verbal aspect. This may be for the best, but there is no doubt that not enough attention has been given to the level of difficulty of the associated language. It can be relatively simple to demonstrate a principle—for example, how a process works, or the properties of a substance—while being very difficult to produce verbally a simple yet accurate symbolic representation. For example, a process such as osmosis in biology can be successfully explained to pupils of ordinary ability with the aid of experiments, diagrammatic representation and even by 'acting out' the process. Remove the visual props and ask your pupils to tell you what happens, or to write down how the process works, and many will start to flounder. The difficulties they experience in finding the right words are not caused only by the employment of technical terms, though some terms like 'semi-permeable membrane' (an understanding of which is essential to an explanation of osmosis) have no easy alternative and have to be grasped. Contributing equally to the difficulty of the task is the necessity for employing syntactic constructions that can carry propositions that are qualified by conditional factors. These are complex constructions often unfamiliar to the pupils because normally their language is rarely called upon to make propositions of this sort with the same degree of conciseness and absence of ambiguity.

Perhaps the most exacting subjects in respect of the difficulties mentioned are physics and chemistry. As has been stressed already, much of the language involved in these subjects has to do with hypothetical and ideal states, which means that the pupil learns to recognise criterial attributes when they occur and to distinguish them from non-criterial attributes. This calls for considerable linguistic skill as on the surface criterial and non-criterial attributes may appear in the same syntactic constructions. The distinctions between them appear in the deep structure of the communication, and therefore the pupil must learn to identify the linguistic pointers at this level if he is to differentiate successfully.

Returning to the subject of the technical term, if the definition of it as a word or phrase which, used in the context of a specific subject, carries a single scientific meaning is acceptable, then indisputably it can make an invaluable contribution to the process of communication between participants who are aware of its meaning. However, the acquisition of these meanings takes time, often much longer than the time taken to acquire the symbolic representation of the meanings—i.e., the words—and both activities demand a conscious effort on the part of the pupil. In certain school subjects, notably at secondary level, pupils are presented with an enormous number of these terms. It is likely that pupils following a biology syllabus leading to the General Certificate of Education at 'O' level will encounter some 1500 technical terms as well as a considerable number of unusual words which do not appear in everyday usage at all frequently. The size of this vocabulary cannot but cause problems even for the more able pupils. It could be reduced by employing ordinary words whenever possible but, again, there is a limit to the extent to which this can be done without loss of accuracy.

Bearing in mind the nature of the difficulties that have been discussed, it does seem very possible that, if too much emphasis, without the accompaniment of verbal formulations and explanations, is placed on practical work, language may be denied opportunities to play its important part in developing concepts. The effects of such impoverishment are very serious. If we accept that to learn a subject is to learn the language of that subject, then it is not only the problem of pupils 'knowing' the concepts of the subject while being unable to express them that is raised. Failure to learn the language retards concept formation to a degree that prevents pupils from making progress in their knowledge and understanding of the subject.

It can, of course, be argued that some pupils are able to pick up the language and manipulate it without having the requisite understanding and others may have more understanding than is manifested by their ability to express it. Teachers are usually well aware of the latter, which occurs quite frequently. They tend to overlook the former because, as mentioned earlier, they assume that, when a pupil uses words and phrases that are appropriate to the subject, his meanings correspond with their own. Both these objections are valid, but they in no way weaken the contention that we can expect pupils who are successfully learning a particular subject to be successfully acquiring its unique language—i.e., the vocabulary, collocations, syntax and style of discourse that are consistent with the role the language has to perform in the context of the subject.

Backing for the contention has been offered in the studies of Taylor (1968) on deep structure in a chemistry text and Evans (1972) on the importance of technical terms. The work of Skemp (1970) on mathematical concepts also lends support with the conclusion that the subject is concerned entirely with concepts and that within hierarchies of concepts we cannot do without words once we have passed the first level. Peel (1970), studying the teaching of history in school, recognises that the subject demands a great deal of conceptual activity from the pupil because of its dependence upon language. Much of the evidence that will be cited in support of the contention, however, is provided from a study by the present writer (Richards, 1974) which attempts to look at the actual process of development of a particular concept in the subject of biology* over a period of ten years, using children in the age range of 7 to 16 years, in order to see if there is any relationship between the maturation of the concept and the acquisition of the language or register of the subject. The question to be answered was: Assuming that subject registers exist in schools, and bearing in mind that thought and language are inextricably bound together, is it necessary for a child learning a subject to acquire its register if he is to achieve understanding and thus knowledge of the subject?

The specific hypotheses* tested were:

1   That there is no direct relationship between the development of accurate biological concepts by a child and his

---

* Biology was considered an ideal choice as it appeals to both arts- and science-oriented pupils.

* For convenience the hypotheses were put in the null form.

acquisition of the register of biology teaching;
2   That there is no relationship between a child's ability to acquire and use the register of biology teaching and his success in the subject as rated by the teacher's assessment.

Ideally, the investigation of these hypotheses would have employed a longitudinal design, starting before the genesis of the particular concept and testing its development at the stages of initial formation of the concept; growth of a spontaneous concept; change from spontaneous to non-spontaneous or scientific and the formation of the mature non-spontaneous or scientific concept. This was never contemplated, for the obvious reason that it would have been necessary to start with children of pre-school age and follow them through to the compulsory school-leaving age. Instead it was decided to concentrate on the period in which a spontaneous concept may develop into a mature non-spontaneous or scientific one, and to emulate the longitudinal design by using equal numbers of children from the year groups 7 to 16. In all, 1000 children were used in the sample, some 100 in each year group.

A questionnaire was constructed to obtain the information. It was necessary that the questions used should be simple enough in form to be understood by pupils as young as 7 years of age, yet allowing for a range of responses such that the scope of pupils of 16 years of age would not be inhibited. The common earthworm was chosen as the subject of the questionnaire for various reasons. It is an organism that will have come to the attention of children at an early age, and therefore some spontaneous concepts will be formed by the age of 7. It is simple enough to allow a measure of non-scientific description, but a full appreciation of its characteristics can only be arrived at through careful observation, taught factual knowledge or experimental investigation or both, and an understanding of biological classification. Also, the earthworm is frequently studied in primary schools and early on in secondary schools in both biology and integrated science courses. A detailed study of the organism is to be found in many examination syllabuses for the Certificate of Secondary Education and at the 'O' level of the General Certificate of Education. In short, it is likely to be a concept with which most children are familiar to some degree.

A picture of the earthworm was given to each pupil together with the questionnaire, the form of which is as follows:

Look at the picture of the specimen—
1 Write down its name.
2 Write down what it looks like so that someone who who could not see or feel it would have an idea of what it was like. List the things below.
3 Write down the name of anything on its body which helps it to move.
4 Write down how it moves.
5 Write down where you would expect to find it.
6 Write down how and what you think it eats.
7 Tick which of the following statements about the specimen is correct:
   (*a*) It is not an animal.
   (*b*) It is a simple animal like a snail
   (*c*) It is a complex animal like a mammal

If you have seen a real snake, or a picture or model of one, answer the next two questions:
8 Write down the ways in which the specimen is like a snake.
9 Write down the ways in which the specimen is not like a snake.
10 Write down the name of the group(s) to which the specimen belongs.

Questions 2-6 inclusive are concerned with the structural and functional characteristics which constitute the nature of the organism. Questions 1, 7, 8, 9 and 10 are concerned with the categorisation of the organism in relation to other living things. Both these elements are integral parts of the complex biological concept of the earthworm. Individual questions concerned with particular aspects of the concept were as follows:

Question 1 tests the acquisition of the naming facility in the pupil, and can be answered generally or scientifically.

Question 2 affords the opportunity for numerous general responses irrespective of the age of the pupil, without precluding responses which would be categorised as intermediate or scientific. The absence of any restriction on the number and variety of possible responses ensures that concrete and abstract notions will be represented.

Question 3 should be answered with an intermediate or scientific concept, because the general concept of a structure associated with movement (legs) is inappropriate in this case.

Question 4 allows responses from all three categories, but accurate responses require an advanced level of conceptual development.

Questions 5 and 6 allow responses from all three categories.

Question 7 has only one scientifically correct response.

Questions 8 and 9 test the attainment by the pupil of a total biological concept of the earthworm by requiring positive and negative instances. Most of the correct examples which can be instanced will be in the intermediate or scientific categories, especially in respect of positive instances.

Question 10 tests the ability of the pupil to place the organism in a class in relation to all living things; it can therefore be answered correctly only with an intermediate or scientific response.

A pilot study was carried out using some 200 pupils in primary and secondary schools to ascertain whether or not schoolchildren aged from 7 to 16 years could complete the questionnaire at a level commensurate with their particular age and development, and whether or not the responses demonstrated a pattern of conceptual development in respect of the particular biological concept. It was also necessary to try to discover any overlooked ambiguities in the wording of the questions.

Each *correct* response elicited by the appropriate question was categorised under one of three headings:

1   A general concept: one which has been acquired spontaneously   and   unconsciously   through   everyday

experiences, but has reached a level of development such that the child is able to define it in words.

2 An intermediate concept: one which has started as a general concept as defined in (1), but which is beginning to absorb a related scientific concept.

3 A scientific concept: one which from its non-spontaneous inception carries the relationship of generality and the beginnings of a system which will be developed by specific teaching and investigation.

The results of the pilot study showed that 85 per cent of the pupils were able to write a response to at least seven questions, although not all responses were correct. The remaining 15 per cent comprised those who attempted fewer than seven questions, those whose answers were unintelligible and those whose writing ability was so limited that their answers had to be transcribed by someone else. As a result of this evidence it was decided to devise a form of procedure that would take account of these problems and also control a possible variable—namely, whether or not the questions are read out to the group by the teacher.

No ambiguities in the questions were revealed by the pilot study, so the form remained the same for the study proper. The questionnaire was then administered to samples of pupils in comprehensive and primary schools in different parts of the country. In the case of the latter, which were in the catchment area of one or other of the comprehensive schools, a printed form of procedure was given to the primary teachers concerned by arrangement with the head of the school. This read:

1 Arrange for members of staff or older pupils to write down the verbal responses of pupils unable to write legibly.

2 Give each child a question sheet and a picture of the specimen.

3 Tell each child to put his/her name in *years* in the space marked.

4 Stress that no one will know which paper is which, they

will not be 'marked', and therefore there is nothing to be gained by copying anyone else.

5 Tell the class that, if they do not know the answer to a question, they should leave it blank and not try to guess it.

6 Read the questions to the class. Take each in turn and give ample time for answers to be written before passing on to the next question.

7 Give any explanation needed to make the meaning of a question clear, but avoid giving clues to the answer.

The schools were also asked to provide information about the ability range of pupils participating in the study. The four categories used were 'below average', 'average', 'above average', 'mixed ability', and if a mixed-ability group, to estimate the range of IQ—e.g., 95-125.

The responses to the questionnaire were categorised in the manner already described and recorded for each question and age group.

As not all the responses could be categorised readily, reliability tests were carried out. The list of the full range of responses made for each question was categorised severally by three biologists. A high degree of agreement was obtained on nearly 90 per cent of the responses, but for the obstinate cases, most of which were concerned with the distinction between intermediate and scientific, a different categorisation could be argued.

Examination of the full range of responses in relation to age, ability and transition from the primary to the secondary stage of education reveals interesting patterns in conceptual development. But as our major concern is with language perhaps the most significant phenomenon is the manner in which the development of the notional aspects of the concept is paralleled by increased use of specialised language which analysis shows to be that associated with the subject. In looking at the examples that will be offered of the numerous instances of this, it should be borne in mind that the choice of language is the pupil's. No attempt was made to influence the range and kind of notions that would be included by pupils or the way in which they would be expressed. Furthermore, a pupil did not obtain a higher score merely by using specialised language. If a notion contributing to the complex concept of an earthworm had been expressed adequately without the use of specialised language, it obtained a score identical to that given when the same notion was expressed in specialised language. Only when the use of specialised language made a notion more specific and accurate or was used to make explicit a notion that had not been offered in non-specialised language did it add to the score of the pupil making the responses to the questions.

One of the clearest patterns that emerges from the results obtained through the questionnaire depicts stages in the development of a biological concept which are related to chronological factors. Thus, leaving aside natural intelligence, children's concepts tend to become broader, deeper and more accurate with age. This is not to say that all children acquire mature concepts at the same age or that the more complex concepts will in time be acquired by all children. The implication is that for children with similar ability any concept acquired at the primary-school stage will have undergone some development by the time the same children reach the end of the secondary-school stage. For example, in answering the second question on the questionnaire (which affords unlimited scope for introducing notions) typical responses from children of average ability are as follows:

At age 7 +   'It is brown, wiggly, it's long.'

At age 10 +   'It is long and thin. It is brown in colour. It has rings round it. It has no eyes. It is slimy.'

At age 12 +   'It is long and thin and brown. It has segments along its body. It has a black patch on it called the saddle. Its skin has rough patches underneath. It is slimy.'

At age 14 +   'It is long thin and brownish in colour. Has segments running along it. Front end is circular and pointed. Back end broad and flattish. Has a broad segment nearer the front end called the saddle. It has small hairs under its body. It is covered with slime. It has a line down its body which is a vein, running from top to bottom.'

At age 16+ 'The earthworm has a body shaped like a closed tube made up of segments or rings which help to make it flexible. The mouth of the animal is at the pointed end—the anus at the flattened end. There is a blood vessel running down the dorsal surface of the animal and visible through the skin. Approximately one third of the body length from the mouth end, is the saddle which is unsegmented. All the body is moist to the touch.'

Whenever the questions afforded a high degree of freedom in respect of possible responses, progressions of the kind seen above were present.

A second factor influencing the stages of development of a concept is the conceptual level demanded by continued expansion of it. This may prove too high for some children at the age at which normally they would be expected to attain it, or may be altogether unattainable. For example, the questions which extracted a large number of correct responses were those which asked for as many concrete notions as possible. Some of these responses could have been utilised in later questions requiring the identification of positive and negative instances in a comparison of the earthworm with a snake. In fact, many children below the age of 11 years were not able to do this successfully, tending to have more difficulty identifying points of similarity (positive instances) than of contrast (negative instances). Another example concerns the questions asking respectively for explanations of how the earthworm moves and feeds. The former proved to be the most difficult for children to answer with any degree of clarity or accuracy. Many offered either no response or an incorrect one. Others used expressions like 'it wriggles along'. To answer the questions correctly pupils had to have attained pre-requisite concepts of muscle function, action of body fluids and pressure, so it was not surprising that adequate responses (those which took some account of the processes involved in the action) were not found below the age of 14 years and were exclusive to the average and above-average groups, being most frequent in the latter. The question on feeding consistently provided responses that demonstrated differences in individual conceptual development associated with ability rather than chronological age. The following examples, which are typical, are drawn from the 14+ age group.

Below-average ability:
   'It eats soil as it goes through the soil.'
Average ability:
   'As it burrows through the soil decayed plant matter is taken in at the front end and passes through the body. Waste is removed at the anus.'
Above-average ability:
   'The earthworm takes in dead vegetation in the soil that enters its mouth as it burrows in the ground. The soil passes down a long tube and the goodness is taken from it leaving the waste which passes out of the anus as worm casts.'

Naming, in the sense of attaching a label to an item, proved to be another activity which in the context of the questionnaire presented no problems to children of the ages represented in the sample. In contrast, placing an item in a class in accordance with the system used in biological classification was beyond most children before the age of 12, and remained unmastered by a considerable number at any age represented in the sample. The latter is particularly noteworthy in the light of the knowledge that from 14+ the majority of pupils in the samples will have chosen to study biology as an examination subject.

Inspection of the categories shows that the rate of growth of the biological concept is not uniform from year to year. The greater advances tend to be associated with specific teaching. For example, the influence of nature study in primary schools would seem to be reflected in the marked increase in intermediate and scientific concepts to be seen around 9 + . The most noticeable change occurs at 12 + and must be accounted for in terms of specialised science teaching in secondary schools. From this point onwards there is a steadier refining and deepening of the concept, although fluctuations still occur which usually can be attributed to the attention the concept is or is not receiving through the teaching which is taking place at the time.

The questions calling forth the purest forms of the register were those which required description of a process or of a structure related to its function. The question concerned with movement that was discussed earlier is an obvious example.

It is difficult to answer with accuracy in a colloquial style because the process is complex and understanding it conceptually demanding. A sizeable minority of pupils did not attempt the question. Of those who did, many gave wrong responses. The remaining correct responses provided a number of significant language progressions. One of the clearest was:

'pulls out and wriggles along'   (general)
'muscles move one end and push the body up
    while the other end gets longer'   (intermediate)
'circular muscles contract exerting pressure
    on body fluids and the body lengthens,
    while longitudinal muscles contract
    and draw up the head region'   (scientific)

Looking at the third response, one of its strengths is the high degree of clarity and specificity that has been achieved. The use of technical terms such as 'circular', 'contract' and 'body fluids' has contributed to this. The response also demonstrates a notable characteristic of the language of science, which is that a great deal of information is carried concisely without loss of accuracy.

The manner in which the language of the responses changes as the concept becomes more scientific is demonstrated again and again in the questionnaire as the responses

are categorised into 'general', 'intermediate' and 'scientific'.
For example, 'a line down it from top to bottom' and 'a line
visible through the skin from anterior to posterior end' are
two statements which are notionally very little different. The
major difference lies in the language used to express the
observation, the second being more readily recognisable as a
piece of scientific information than the first. Such examples
are common, the more 'extreme' cases of the biological
register being present in the responses of the 14+ to 16+
groups:

> 'draws food through the sucker into the gullet'
> 'absence of a distinct head, trunk and tail region, and
> highly developed sense organs'.

Clearly, the nature of the question exerts its own influence
on the sort of language produced. As was explained in the
design of the research, certain questions required a range of
responses which would include general concepts. These
questions called forth the largest proportion of non-
specialised language, much of which was conceptually
categorised as general or intermediate. The related scientific
categories do show distinctive language features, the most
prominent being the use of technical terms. The following
example is typical:

> 'a squashy body'   (general)
> 'a body with no bones'   (intermediate)
> 'a body without a skeletal system' (scientific)

In respect of progressions present in the responses, of
which the ones described above are typical, it appears that a
greater advance has been made in the move from general to
intermediate concepts than in the move from intermediate to
scientific ones, but that the move from intermediate to
scientific demonstrates a bigger advance in the development
of specialised language, which has the effect of making the
response more clearly defined. Inspection of precise and
accurate scientific responses made by pupils over the total

sample indicates that those who offered a large number of these were predominantly users of the specialised language associated with the subject of biology. Thus, it would seem that there is a stage in the process of learning a subject at which, to be able to refine a concept and present it with the minimum of ambiguity while at the same time keeping it reasonably concise, it is necessary to use the language forms that have come about in response to the demand for just these same functions. In other words, the appropriate variety for the subject, where appropriate, in this context means the language that can accommodate the functions described. Furthermore, if this facility promotes learning, we can expect pupils who do well in a subject at school to be users of its specialised language.

At this stage it was decided to test out the last hypothesis by asking teachers to indicate ability in the subject for individual pupils in small samples and to compare the rating with the concept score and use of specialised language of the same pupils as indicated by the questionnaire. The work of all the pupils rated was well known to the teachers concerned, and account was taken of past performance over a period of two years. General ability as indicated by intelligence tests was controlled by matching the groups. Once the ratings of high, average or low ability in the subject were obtained for each pupil, they were set beside the pupil's responses to the questionnaire.

Certain correlations were obtained. There is considerable agreement between all three at the high end of the assessment scale. The low end of ability shows a perfect correlation between teacher's rating and that for use of specialised language, but some pupils have a higher concept level than is indicated by the teacher's rating or the register score. Just one pupil had a high success rating, a high concept level and only an average language score. Over all there is more agreement between use of specialised language and teachers' rating than between concept level and teachers' rating. Furthermore, at the high-assessment end there is closer agreement between use of specialised language and concept level than between concept level and teachers' rating. For the same comparison at the low end, the agreement is the same in both instances.

The evidence supports the contention that the subject language or register is an important influence for success in the subject, both for its influence on concept development and on the impression a pupil gives of his ability in school, and thus in practice should feed attainment as clearly as possible.

In the case of the impression given to teachers by use of register, they believe a concept to be more adequately expressed when the language used is specialised rather than non-specialised. Rightly or wrongly, they have reason to make this assumption as public examination boards reinforce the belief, not only in what they reward with marks, but in their own choice of the language in which they couch the questions asked.

Before discussing the implications of the evidence, it may be helpful to have a summary of all the points mentioned in the results. The development of a scientific concept in a subject such as biology shows progressions with age and learning (i.e., specific subject teaching). The progression is from limited concepts to richer, broader, deeper ones; from spontaneous or general concepts through an intermediate stage to non-spontaneous or scientific concepts; from a number of 'false' concepts to increasingly correct and accurate ones.

The development of the unique language or register of the subject shows a corresponding progression. From simple language to more complex forms; from a language without special vocabulary and formal structures to one that makes increasing use of technical terms and the syntactic structures associated with scientific English.

Successful acquisition and use of the subject register correlates positively with the development of accurate biological concepts and success in the subject as assessed by teachers.

In looking at the implications of the results, it is necessary to remember that the past half-century has seen many changes in methods of teaching, and in no field is this truer than that of biology. From a situation where biology was taught by bookish methods, there has been a move through the stage of observation and drawing to active laboratory work.

It would be reasonable to suppose that experimental and other practical activities have reduced the reliance upon verbal explication. At first glance this may appear to be the case, for there is often a great deal of moving about taking place in school laboratories, and the level of noise is not conducive to careful deductive discussion at this stage. Obviously, time should be allocated at some stage for this purpose but, as time is limited and syllabuses remain large, descriptive language often is cut back. Discovery methods increase the need for a pupil to use language to record, define and hypothesise, for these are the functions associated with the scientific activities that new methods are attempting to emulate. However, because practical work is generally more time-consuming than a theoretical approach pupils may have to cope with the language aspect of the work for themselves simply because there is not time within the lesson to give it much attention. It is also true that textbooks designed for use with methods of teaching involving inquiry tend to ask questions in the text rather than supply statements of fact. This may have advantages in relation to the pupil's ability to think for himself, but it removes a possible language model that could help the pupil to become familiar with the language of the subject. Add to this the effects of the tendency among teachers using discovery methods to give short introductions and expositions or, indeed, to leave them out altogether, and the net result is that many pupils may get little support in meeting demands on their language that are heavier than those made by traditional methods.

This is not to say that pupils being taught science subjects by traditional methods are necessarily better able to acquire the language of the subject, and thus the concepts of the subject, than those taught by discovery methods. However, evidence from a study carried out by the present writer (Richards, 1971), in which the effectiveness of discovery and traditional methods of teaching biology were compared, pointed to traditional methods as being more effective with pupils of average and below average language competence.

The success of discovery methods appeared to be greatly influenced by the level of language competence—i.e., it was as effective as, and at times marginally more effective than, traditional methods with pupils having a high level of language competence.

Irrespective of the method used to teach pupils a subject, the test of their success in learning what has been taught is still likely to be an examination of some sort. A significant report by O'Donnell (1967) on the role of language at Scottish 'O' Grade identifies an effect upon performance of inadequate subject language. The subject he investigated is physics and his results are summarised as follows:

(a) Choice of question does not appear to be significantly related to ability to do the question.
(b) There is a positive relationship between questions most frequently chosen and those which were least syntactically complex.
(c) There is some negative relationship between questions in which candidates performed best and those which were least syntactically complex.
(d) There is fairly conclusive evidence to suggest that vocabulary weakness could affect the range of choice offered by the questions and the performance of the candidate on a considerable scale.

Perhaps the largest cause of the problems that have been described stem from the fact that there is an unconscious element in much language behaviour that strengthens the likelihood that many teachers will be unaware of their subject-language use and more specifically of the linguistic features characteristic of it. Because of this they may not realise that the level of language development demanded by certain registers may be more advanced than the conceptual level of the topic being taught, thus causing pupils to have greater difficulty with the language than with the concept itself. Equally possible is the situation which has been discussed earlier, where pupils pick up the register piecemeal and find that to produce a fragment correctly from time to time, often in response to questions from the teacher requiring short answers, obtains rewards more surely than do their attempts to verbalise in their own style. This activity on the part of the pupil is associated with his effort to acquire the language of the subject and is therefore necessary. The danger lies in a teacher's assumption that correct use of subject register implies acquisition of the concept, for this need not be the case.

For those concerned with the education of children, the most obvious implication suggested by the examples is that the language of learning needs to be simplified. While it is true that there is much unnecessary complication of language that could and should be checked, it is unlikely that the solution to the problem for the pupil is the removal of subject registers. The justification for this view is that registers are not unnecessary artifices or irresponsible fashions. They have risen gradually and naturally in response to the demands made upon language by the functions language has and is being called upon to perform. They are directly related to the range and variety of the concepts contained in a culture.

It would seem highly appropriate for pupils to become acquainted with some of the different language forms that exist in their society, especially as the *forms* associated with what we call 'subjects' (i.e., areas of study concerned with making sense of the various phenomena of this world) are crucial to the accurate expression, definition and conveyance of subject concepts which are the basis of our understanding of things. Indeed, an extension of the first implication is that a repertoire of language varieties is central to learning processes in school and raises two important questions which will be given further attention in the final chapter. These are:

1 How do pupils learn the language of learning?
2 Is it possible to improve a pupil's repertoire of language varieties by the use of specific strategies and techniques?

Answers to these questions are important, for they are the key to making a pupil's language a rich and adaptable instrument for his use.

Chapter 6

Some Conclusions and Recommendations

In the previous chapters we have examined notions and theories concerned with understanding more about the nature and function of language behaviour, and also evidence provided by studies in which samples of language in use in 'live' situations concerned with the teaching and learning of concepts associated with a variety of school subjects have been obtained and analysed.

Few undisputed conclusions emerge, which will afford little surprise for those who have come to realise how great are the odds against making any definitive statement about language that is adequate to take account of its complex, intangible and dynamic characteristics. However, the realisation is itself a valuable outcome of the exercise if it protects us from falling into the same trap as those who, failing to appreciate the diversity of phenomena represented in the term 'language', seek a comprehensive explanation within a single model. At best the evidence that we have examined can do no more than add to our knowledge and hopefully to our understanding of the range of functions and experiences for which and in which language is a fundamental factor. Furthermore, it is likely that future knowledge—be it the fruits of conjecture or of objective research—will also come to us piecemeal, because any rigorous work in this vast field has of necessity to be confined to a small, clearly defined area.

The problem does not end with the gathering of evidence. That which is uncovered through studies still has to be interpreted if we are desirous of applying the knowledge gained to language use and practices in the classroom. This is now the concern of many teachers who, as a result of the explosion of interest in this topic, have become increasingly aware that language plays a vital central role in school learning.

But to which area of the wide field that falls within the scope of language should they give particular attention, and upon which interpretation of available evidence should they pin their faith? These are crucial questions, and the individual teacher's response to them will influence his attitudes and actions in the classroom. For instance, if he has accepted uncritically any interpretation as giving the 'one true explanation' of language behaviour, it is all too easy for him unconsciously to identify phenomena that corroborate and reinforce the line of thought he has accepted, while remaining oblivious of other phenomena that question or contradict it—a state of affairs that comes about the more readily when the issues involved have parallels in the political, cultural or ideological controversies going on within our society. For example, views of language behaviour based on social class have been seized upon and broadcast widely. Professional conferences take them up as themes, colleges of education include them in their courses, pressure groups of all kinds use them in support of such demands as increased provision of different kinds, de-schooling, and positive discrimination in favour of the underprivileged. The 'ordinary' teacher has his attention drawn to them through in-service courses, talks at teachers' centres and a mass of literature pointing out the failure of the schools to educate the working-class child satisfactorily.

Widespread 'publicity' for a specific viewpoint will tend to exaggerate its degree of importance and the impact it has relative to any other that has not been given the same treatment. In addition, with so much being written and said, by the time the messages of the latest research studies have reached the rank and file tentative conclusions and possible implications have somewhere along the line become firm statements and proven facts—and you cannot argue with these! Let us therefore consider one or two current interpretations of language behaviour with a view to offering to teachers recommendations concerning, on the one hand, stances to be avoided as language-limiting and, on the other, what seems to be 'good practice' in the light of available evidence—bearing in mind that such recommendations as are made will not necessarily be those other writers in the field would offer.

LANGUAGE BEHAVIOUR AND SOCIAL FACTORS

It is possible, because social factors so obviously influence language behaviour (and, indeed, some would define language as social behaviour), that socio-linguistic studies, with certain notable exceptions, have shown less interest in the possible links between an individual's language behaviour and his life-style (both of which are influenced further by intellectual and personality factors) than they have in establishing correlations between language behaviour and social-class membership. Nor can this pre-occupation be defended adequately on the grounds that the factors involved sometimes turn out to be the same in the final analysis. For, while this may be true for certain individuals in each of the social-class categories, it is demonstrably untrue for others. Thus, we will come no nearer to identifying the crucial factors unless we look for these influences within an individual's life-style and not in groups that have been defined on the basis of somewhat arbitrary criteria.

Although many studies have attempted to expose the influence of social background, the socio-linguistic notions of Bernstein (as has been shown already) have attained great prominence, centring as they do upon social-class models of socialisation as the major influence upon the sort of language a child develops, and linking these with success or failure (depending upon the class) in school. Nor is the social-class stereotypes model much challenged by those who more recently have been critical of Bernstein's work. Devotees of Labov use the class stereotypes to argue that *working-class* language is as 'good' as *middle-class* language, and that learning problems arise for the working-class child because his culture is not sufficiently represented in the activities of the school.

Numerous other contentions and criticisms of the sort

described abound in articles and books concerned with the influence of social background upon educability. While not wishing to denigrate the contribution of those working in this field, it does seem that in far too much of what is written (perhaps in the heat generated by sociological or political axe-grinding or both) class stereotypes appear as 'real' categories. It is therefore hardly surprising that teachers and students training for teaching, reading such articles, follow the lead of the writers and also accept the class cleavage as absolute.

However, as we are not behavioural scientists under pressure to identify generalised behaviour within society, but teachers concerned with individuals, we can start by questioning the *usefulness* of class and language stereotypes on the grounds that

(a) Individuals in complex societies are members of more than one group, and this will involve them in the use of a range of different kinds of language.

(b) Stereotypes cannot adequately accommodate the dynamic properties of either social class or language behaviour.

(c) Readily identifiable types are likely to be found in small minority groups at the extreme opposite ends of a continuum, and it follows that any attempt to classify the characteristics of the language of groups as amorphous and ill defined as those in our society that we refer to as working-class and middle-class respectively is unlikely to produce anything more subtle and useful than the rather crude stereotypes which we now have.

If as teachers we still think that it is helpful to our understanding of language to look for typical features related to class, then surely the concern should be with finding out more about the number of distinctive forms of language an individual has at his command. This means we need something like Fishman's (1970) concept of repertoire range in order to try to determine how much of the entire speech community's verbal repertoire is available to the numerous smaller interaction networks within it. Also (as has already been stated) all individuals are members of more than one group and thus members of more than one speech network. The functions of the language employed in these networks depend upon the norms of the group generating them. The norms in turn adapt when necessary to changes within the group in response to circumstances, group concepts and interaction with other groups. In consequence: 'All varieties of all languages are equally expendable and changeable; all are equally contractable and interpenetrable under the influence of foreign models' (Fishman, 1970).

The same dynamic quality can be recognised in the individual's facility for switching from one kind of language to another in response to the pressure of a new situation or topic with its own peculiar linguistic demands. The language of individuals who have a wide variety of life experiences is likely to be more adaptable and thus more dynamic than that of others whose experiences are limited, while the largest linguistic repertoires are to be found in speech networks that have a wide range of expectation, interaction with other networks, and interesting specialisations of all types. The implication for the teacher of these arguments is that life experience is a more reliable guide to the language ability of pupils than their social-class membership, and even for the clearly identifiable class types what is designated *typically* working-class or middle-class speech should not be so judged on *unique* features of the language form. If it is to take any account of the way in which language functions naturally in the entire speech community, the 'typical' must refer to repertoire range.

This makes the use of terms such as 'inadequate' or 'deprived' in relation to an individual's *total* language very suspect. If such terms are to be used accurately, then they are acceptable only on the occasions when a piece of language fails to operate successfully in a situation in which a member of a group wishes to participate.

The objections that have been discussed support the suggestion that teachers could usefully set aside stereotypes which depend upon attempts to identify typical linguistic characteristics of entire speech networks and concentrate on the notion of repertoire range to explain distinctions among children with regard to their language behaviour. Not only can the concept be usefully employed in this way, but it would also seem on available evidence to offer a more satisfactory explanation of apparent inadequacies in language than does a language-deprivation theory, which by its very title implies a totality which is often misleading and, indeed, at times false.

If the teacher lays aside class stereotypes, to what factors can he look to enable him to gauge the language competence and weaknesses of the members of his class? Can he in fact make any assumptions about what to expect?

In the first place, barring gross abnormalities, every child arrives at school with a language system of some kind. As the sequence of appearance of language behaviour seems to be the same for all children* and, as has been argued, they have come into contact with more than one language variety, it follows that each child has a repertoire—though ranges will differ with regard to their width in relation to factors such as:

(a) The richness and variety of experiences in which the child has actually participated;

(b) The range of language models that the child has heard spoken;

(c) The opportunities afforded the child to 'practise' different kinds of language through natural usage;

(d) The intellectual ability of the child in relation to items like intelligent behaviour, perception and memory;

(e) The personality of the child in relation to factors like extroversion versus introversion and anxiety versus confidence.

Within this framework it may be possible to identify almost as many differences among members of the same class as exist between the two class stereotypes that we have put to one side.

* E. H. Lenneberg, *Biological Foundations of Language* (New York: Wiley, 1967)

The first three items listed are social factors likely to affect the life-style of individuals. Looking at each in turn, the first (relating to differences in experience) immediately presents us with the problem of interpreting what is to be considered *valuable*. By and large, this difficulty is resolved through the dubious practice of employing subjective judgements which tend to reflect the social conditioning of the adult making the judgement. Where this is the case the adult is always in danger of assuming the commonplace experiences of today's children to be those of his own childhood, and may decide that a particular child's experience is limited on the basis of this assumption. For example, Creber (1972) describes his amazement upon discovering that a Birmingham 9-year-old had never seen a railway station. Yet this plight is increasingly common with the tendency for 'new schools' to take children from the immediate neighbourhood—i.e., within walking-distance—the closure of many stations and, most significant of all, the use of cars for transporting children to school, on visits and trips and for family holidays.

We could also question whether alleys, patches of waste ground and industrial landscapes should be considered less stimulating and interesting as 'play environments' than the tiny gardens in neat but dull rows of streets that are so typical of modern private housing-estates—many of which have fewer play areas provided than do the council-owned estates, and these have few enough. The point made is not intended to be seen as an attempt to justify inadequate housing; it simply challenges the assumptions that we have of what constitutes a stimulating environment, assumptions that are made on the basis of *adult* subjective judgements of what a *child* perceives as an interesting and exciting environment.

Children who go out often with their parents are said to have opportunities to avail themselves of experiences denied to others, who are left to their own devices or with siblings and peers. But, again, if we are prepared to put aside any preconceived notions and set the advantages of the former—i.e., having outings directed towards objectives defined by the adult (which thus *may* have greater educational content)—beside the advantages of the latter—i.e., being able to explore as personal curiosity dictates and to learn to look after oneself in the process—it is no easy task to decide which is the more valuable experience.

Clearer distinctions exist among children in respect of the influence of the different kinds of language that a child hears spoken in his everyday life. Indeed, this factor is influential in the early stages of language development in that it prepares the child in advance for new and complex structures and reinforces in the period when the child is acquiring and developing them. It is important that teachers appreciate the effects of this factor upon children's language and do not jump to the conclusion that the child with a limited range has an inadequate language system. Given opportunities to hear and practise different varieties through use, the range can be developed and thus language ability improved.

Can this be what is sought by recommendation 110 of the Bullock Report (1974) in relation to what is called 'a language for life'? The recommendation states that:

Children should be helped to as wide as possible a range of language uses so that they can speak appropriately in different situations and use standard forms when they are needed.

It is to be hoped that it will be interpreted as meaning that every individual needs a repertoire containing a number of different kinds of language, that ideally his range should cover all the language activities in which he is likely to want or need to participate, that in school he should be helped to attain the range he needs by being given opportunities to learn and practise new forms that are appropriate to the functional demands made by differing intellectual and social situations. It is also to be hoped that teachers will not take too narrow a view of the kind of range a pupil needs to suit his life-style. It would be disastrous if too little of the speech community's repertoire were made available to pupils from less favourable backgrounds. The aim should be to widen the scope of their language behaviour, and this cannot be done on a diet of educational experiences that take them no further than their own front doors.

LANGUAGE BEHAVIOUR AND PERSONALITY FACTORS

The influence of personality factors upon language behaviour can be easily overlooked in the assessment of language ability on the basis of children's speech acts. The behavioural expectations of many primary schools have more in common with the natural behaviour of the extrovert personality than with that of the introvert. Indeed, the language environment tends to develop extroversion. Talk is rewarded even when irrelevant to the topic, and a strong emphasis is placed upon the verbalisation of personal experience and opinion. The move to the secondary sector must therefore be an unsettling experience for most pupils and even traumatic for some. In no area must greater adaptation take place than in relation to the language environment of the secondary school—from a situation in the primary school where talk is welcomed for its own sake, and the introvert under pressure to conform to extrovert norms of language activity, to a new situation in which almost the opposite language behaviour is expected.

It is now the extrovert who is under pressure to conform to norms of language behaviour which are at variance with his personality. In many ways he may be worse off than the introvert in the primary school, for it is more difficult for him to adapt at this later stage, especially as his natural language activity has been reinforced by its success in the primary sector. There is no doubt that this state of affairs can undermine the confidence of children, and their achievements suffer in consequence.

Using evidence from the present writer's study described in the previous two chapters, a description of the secondary-school language environment can be built up. It is helpful to distinguish social and intellectual activity and to describe each separately, but the two categories must not be thought of as existing separately in reality.

Most secondary schools can be thought of as large units, and compared with primary schools they are *very* large units. They are organised in such a way that children meet a number of different teachers during a school day. Close personal relationships between pupils and teachers of the sort that can be developed in the primary school are rarely possible. Indeed, the true state of affairs is much worse than this. Many secondary teachers get a sense of achievement if they can put names to the faces of *all* the pupils they teach. The position improves as pupils spend more time with teachers of subject choices further up the school, but is at its worst in the first two years.

The situation has a marked effect upon social language activity in the school. The casual language of intimates, characterised by a warm, easy, colloquial, personal style, gives way to ceremonial forms that are felt to be more appropriate to the relationships possible between secondary teachers and most first- and second-year pupils. This is characterised by increased use of polite forms of address and changes in the language of ordinary conversations towards careful, deferential and formal style—particularly on the part of the pupil towards the teacher. Demands are frequently replaced by requests. This is noticeable in the social-control questions used by teachers in the sample lessons in the study.* For example, 'If you don't finish your work you will stay in at break to do so,' is replaced by 'You don't want to stay in at break to finish the work, do you?' Social-appeal questions show the same trend—'Wash your hands before you go to lunch' being replaced by 'Now, you won't forget to wash your hands before lunch, will you?'

The shortage of social questions in the lessons, other than social control and social appeal (and these are few enough), is particularly significant. Five subjects had no such questions asked in the five lessons taped for each subject, while English with the highest recorded number of questions has an average of only three per lesson. One of the explanations of this phenomenon given by teachers is that they feel they are struggling against time in their efforts to cover the work dictated by the syllabus which they are following. This encourages them to avoid 'wasting' time in the lesson on topics that are not directly related to the work in hand. This helps to explain the distinction between English and most

* Richards, 1974.

other subjects with regard to social questions; i.e., in some English lessons the nature of the topic is such as to encourage social discourse.

The lack of social discourse in lessons has a more generalised effect upon the language behaviour in the classroom. The signals from the teacher may imply that what can be offered spontaneously by the child, especially in relation to personal experience, is deemed irrelevant and in some cases unwelcome. Although teachers may not be aware of the extent to which they take over the major part of the discourse (often two-thirds of the talk in the lesson is the teacher's, which leaves a relatively small amount to be spread among thirty pupils), the pupils cannot help but get the message that what can be and is said is decided by the teacher. Commonly, teachers phrase statements and questions in a way that provides small gaps to be filled in by the pupils with what the teacher juges to be the 'right' response. This almost total absence of a social context from which the pupil can operate (it being a very familiar context) and, indeed, venture forth with confidence into unfamiliar contexts, such as those provided by the specialist language of certain subjects, hinders pupils in various ways. They will find it difficult to initiate discussion with the teacher, to question things they do not understand, to think their way through a problem 'aloud'. It may also alter their perception of the teacher in a way which would be considered undesirable, setting up anxiety in some and antipathetic feelings in others. 'Threatened' extroverts may seek to regain their status with peers and the teacher by 'clowning' or some other kind of attention-seeking behaviour and shy or anxious children refrain from making any verbal contribution in class, especially when they feel uncertain about a piece of knowledge.

Teachers want to establish a good working relationship with their pupils so that they can co-operate with one another in the learning process. The obvious way to build this is to use social relationships as the foundation, especially with pupils who have recently transferred from a situation in which the social context has been given a very prominent position as an initiator of speech acts. The advantages to be gained are not only that pupils find the ethos of the classroom to be secure and friendly, thus making it possible for them to make headway in social interaction with each other and the teacher, but also that it is possible for them to make mistakes and admit to ignorance without the loss of face that can be so damaging to a child's self-image and thus to his progress in the learning of skills and subject disciplines.

While observation of *primary* classrooms may lead to the conclusion that social discourse is welcome—and this is highly desirable—there are some cautionary points that should be made. Because of distinctions related to both intellectual and personality factors, some children have the capacity and the inclination to spend at least as much time on being an *active* listener and possibly thinker as they do on actual speaking. Primary teachers, therefore, should guard against any misguided inclination to *force* 'natural' listeners or thinkers into undertaking more often the role of a speaker. The importance for language development of attentive listening has been underrated in the past and may go some way towards explaining the commonly made but mistaken assumption that children who talk a great deal are also highly successful in operating a range of language skills. This may or may not be the case, but in the absence of evidence to support the assumption that a direct relationship exists it is safer to consider the amount of talking that a child engages in spontaneously as much a reflection of personality factors as it is of language ability, and to modify action accordingly.

Taking account of normal distinctions among children with regard to the amount of speaking which they choose to do, the job of the primary teacher is to try to ensure that ample opportunity for listening and speaking are given. Ideally, each child is able to speak when he feels he has something to say, and no utterances are cut short or received without due respect.

Bearing in mind that the aim of the teacher is the improvement of language skills, quantity alone is not enough. It is the *extension* of language that is crucial to the perfecting of old skills and the acquisition of new ones. Perhaps equally important, attentive listening must be rewarded as liberally as effective speech, for listening is as vital as speaking if the spontaneous, often disjointed and ego-centric utterances of the younger child are to develop into verbal interaction involving activities such as arguing, explaining, discussing and holding meaningful conversations. It goes without saying that secondary teachers must also share some of the responsibility for providing an ethos that is less anxiety-producing. This could be done by making greater use of language in social contexts so that any language confidence that has been developed at the primary stage is not dissipated but built upon as a sound foundation for new structures.

LANGUAGE BEHAVIOUR AND CONCEPTUAL FACTORS

To a considerable extent intellectual activity in the secondary school goes on within subject disciplines and the language in the secondary classroom is influenced by factors other than those related to the personality and teaching style of the teacher. Thus, another group of considerations, not discussed in the section on social language, comes into play. In the first place different subjects make different kinds of demand upon pupils, and pupils are expected to come to terms with the expectations peculiar to each subject. For example, it was noticeable in the figures recorded for each subject in the question analysis of the present writer's study (Richards, 1974) that some subjects are predominantly concerned with the transmission of a large body of facts from teacher to pupil and others with recalled and sometimes unrecalled reasoning. Open questions in which the pupil really has a choice of responses—in the way he frequently had in the primary classroom—are now rarer. It is also rare to find a teacher asking a question of a pupil because he, the teacher, does not know the answer to it. In a great many cases where factual and reasoning recalled questions are asked by teachers, if we can trust the teacher's response, more praise is given for responses that are couched in the language variety of the subject—even in cases where this is nothing more than the use of a technical term or a definition. Pupils struggling to explain things in their own words may well be given the impression that they are holding things up.

Pupils who fail to perceive the change in the learning environment—and these will tend to be those with the narrowest ranges of language—continue to use the language variety most familiar to them, which in the new context may be deemed inappropriate. Not only does this gain less reward from the teacher, but it can also be as inadequate for carrying the meaning intended as the teacher's language variety sometimes is for carrying his meaning to certain pupils. If the style of language is particularly difficult, confused pupils rationalise in an effort to restore confidence. The subject is too difficult; they don't like it; they don't like the teacher; they don't need the subject anyway. Whatever the reason given, they give up trying to make sense of their experience in this context and thus fail to learn what the teacher is trying to teach them. The situation is one of the few in school of which it can be said that the pupils are 'lost for words' (after Creber, 1972). But even this should be qualified, for they are not really lost for words; rather they are lost for the *right* words. They have found themselves in a situation where their language, which may have served them well hitherto, has broken down.

It is not only children with narrow repertoire ranges to whom this happens when in the secondary school they are first faced with the language of subject specialisation. Obviously, children with a wide repertoire backed up by a high level of ability adapt fairly quickly to the new forms. But what of the others? Will they be left to 'give up' the subject because they don't like it, cannot do it, don't like the teacher, etc., when the real problem is that their own familiar language has ceased to function adequately? The answer largely depends upon the *awareness* of teachers in respect of their own language behaviour and the differences in respect of range represented within the group of pupils they teach.

For most subject learning it is very important that language development is judged in relation to repertoire. A look at the records to check the spread of reading-ages in a class or group is not enough—even if this information is available. This is because a child may be successful in one language situation, and markedly unsuccessful in another demanding quite different linguistic skills. Bearing this in mind, it would be reasonable to expect teachers of science subjects to make the assumption that most of their first-year pupils will be unfamiliar with even the simplest variety of scientific English found in elementary texts and attempt to modify the problem by planning their introduction of specialist language as carefully as they plan the context of the lesson to take account of different levels of conceptual difficulty. However, examination of the language of the twenty-five science lessons obtained for the present writer's study (1974) did not reveal any *systematic* attempt on the part of most of the teachers of science who participated to do this, although there is evidence that some of them are more aware of their language behaviour than others.

The most common indicators of a teacher's awareness of his own language behaviour and the potential difficulties for the pupil of the subject register identified in the study are:

(*a*)   Explanation of the meaning of technical terms (though this was sometimes done using other words almost as difficult and unfamiliar);

(*b*)   Use of relatively short sentences;

(*c*)   Repetition of sentences carrying important basic concepts;

(*d*)   The expansion of definitions using simpler language;

(*e*)   The use of simpler language in explanations.

It is perhaps significant that the last item cited—i.e., the use of simpler forms of language in explanations—is in most cases accomplished through the use of an analogy with an everyday phenomenon. Whenever this is done, the language used to describe the examples from the everyday context becomes—appropriately, we would suggest—more personal and colloquial in style.

Specialised language couched in a formal and complex style occurs in the lessons of most subjects in the sample and notably in physics, chemistry, biology and physical geography. Particularly common is the avoidance of personal language and use of passive rather than active verb forms. There are times when these features are serving a useful purpose, but other times when the only obvious explanation of their use is that the teacher has himself become locked in the language behaviour of his subject. In such cases he appears unconscious of this and equally unconscious of the fact that he is not communicating with his pupils because very few can understand what it is he is trying to say.

There are also numerous examples of what Barnes calls the 'language of secondary education' again in all but a few of the forty-five lessons analysed in the study. This register differs from specialised forms such as scientific English in one fundamental respect—namely, that it is *not* serving a useful function. This register, with its affinity with the rather formal, pompous style of public statements and announcements often associated with bureaucracy, is being used in a context which does not demand it. Why teachers choose to use language of this kind is uncertain. In some cases it may have to do with a teacher's perception of his role; i.e., he feels he is imparting knowledge and that this demands a 'suitable' pedagogic style. Others may feel a sense of insecurity in relation to teaching pupils concepts which perhaps they themselves find difficult to understand, and therefore use the 'public' style as a prop.*

Whatever the explanation for all the questions that have been raised about language behaviour in the classroom, my study supplies indisputable evidence of distinctions between one subject and another in relation to their intrinsic natures and associated activities. Thus, although all subjects share common elements associated with learning, they do differ with regard to the kind of conceptual and linguistic demands that each makes upon the pupil. Such distinctions as are identified in the study can only be accommodated readily if the pupil's repertoire range contains at least the rudimentary structure consistent with the different varieties of language

---

* This possibility can also be considered in relation to teachers who appear to experience difficulty in departing from the specialised language of their subject—notably students and first-year teachers.

represented. Very few children are likely to be in this position at entry into the secondary school, and thus the onus is firmly upon the school to tackle the problem of assisting pupils to acquire the new varieties.

There are good linguistic reasons for acquiring and developing several varieties, for the greater the range the more flexible and adaptable the language. In simple terms, this means that the individual can do more with it. However, evidence from the studies of Evans (1972) and Taylor (1968) and the present writer (1974) supports the contention that in the learning situation the specialised language of a subject *can* be inextricably bound up with its notions as conveyed in the concepts. One cannot learn one without the other.

To summarise some examples of this, Evans (1972) identifies the function of the technical term as being concerned with facilitating precise, clear, unambiguous communication, because it carries one unmistakable meaning for those who have acquired it in a specific context. Taylor (1968), concentrating on the deep structure of texts, demonstrates how linguistic structures function as indicators of criterial attributes in relation to particular phenomena, and the present writer's results show a correlation between well-developed use of a subject's register and successful acquisition of its concepts. Thus, the gains to be had from extending repertoire range include increased language potential and facilitating conceptual learning of all kinds, but specifically non-spontaneous concepts. These are those concepts which do not arise spontaneously in ordinary everyday experience but need to be presented usually through verbal formulations. They are the concepts which abound in the knowledge taught in secondary schools within the subject disciplines.

It would obviously be helpful to teachers to know more about the relationship of language to thought and, indeed, something of the way in which this relationship is manifested linguistically. Such knowledge would form the basis of a conscious effort to adapt the language of learning to accommodate both those who have the rudiments of appropriate structures and those who have to start from scratch and acquire a register that may have the opposite stylistic features to those associated with familiar, colloquial and personal language.

There are crucial questions to be considered before we can agree on a systematic method of tackling the problem. A number of these are concerned with what constitutes adequate language development in present-day society. The Bullock Committee has spent a considerable time on such questions, and it is therefore helpful to look at some of the recommendations which it has arrived at after taking account of a great many differing views. Below are given some of the recommendations that have particular relevance for the issues that have been discussed here. The number of the recommendation is that of the Bullock Report (1974), but the recommendations have been regrouped by the present writer so that those referring to a specific issue are together.

The need for some general language policy:

4 Each school should have an organised policy for language across the curriculum, establishing every teacher's involvement in language and reading development throughout the years of school.*

6 There should be closer consultation between schools and the transmission of effective records, to ensure continuity in the teaching of reading and in the language development of every pupil.*

8 Every L.E.A. should appoint a specialist English adviser and should establish an advisory team with the specific responsibility of supporting schools in all aspects of language in education.*

15 A substantial course on language in education (including reading) should be part of every primary and secondary school teacher's initial training, whatever the teacher's subject or the age of the children with whom he or she will be working.

---

* These recommendations are taken from the list of *principal* recommendations. All others are from the full list of conclusions and recommendations.

A glance at the recommendations makes clear the point that the Bullock Report is not exclusively concerned with the teaching of English as a subject, but that it covers every aspect of language in all sectors of education. It has something to say to teachers regardless of the age range of the pupils they teach or the subject field. Indeed, by urging a language policy in schools across the curriculum the hope is surely that teachers will be made aware both of the common concerns that arise from the use of language in social and learning situations and of the special linguistic demands of specific subject areas.

Sensibly, teacher-training is seen as having a role to play in bringing about the recommendations through inclusion in the course-work in colleges of education of studies relating to the use of language in school. Nor does the committee see such studies as optional for students but rather as a basic and necessary part of the preparation to all recruits to the profession. However effective this action eventually proves to be in producing teachers who are aware of language in the context of learning, it will obviously take some time for these measures to make a noticeable impact upon practice. Thus, if any of the recommendations is to be implemented without considerable delay, the co-operation of the mass of the teaching profession is needed. This means that teachers are being called upon to get to know more about the way they use language in their classrooms, more about the relationship between the notional and verbal aspects of concepts, more about the contribution to educational failure that is made by presenting pupils with excessive linguistic demands. In other words, they need to gain an appreciation of the repertoire that a pupil needs in order to function adequately as a learner and a person at each stage in the process of education within the education system of this country.

An appreciation of the kind described would almost certainly call for some rethinking of our ideas about the functions of language in a variety of contexts and the timing of the development of special forms that are needed to take account of these functions. For example, teachers in the primary sector who may have an aversion to language forms with any formal characteristics on the grounds that these are out of place in the world of the primary-aged child will need to modify this stance. The models of language that children are internally motivated to acquire from birth are always markedly in advance of their need and ability to use them. Clearly, the secondary sector is concerned with some activities that require formal structures, and thus if primary education is but one stage in an ongoing process, then it must have some concern for the future needs of the child as well as for his present needs.

The secondary schools must also play their part in making the transition from the relatively more personal informal and colloquial style of discourse found in primary-school classrooms to subject styles with characteristics of the opposite kind more comfortable and comprehensible for pupils. Specialist language would have to be properly introduced and explained, and in the early years kept down to the minimum necessary to the adequate expressing of the concepts of the subject. Both the primary and secondary sectors would have to banish the belief that *one* variety of language is 'better' than any other and the attempt to make this single variety fit all the very different situations that arise in school. To try to do this is to deny the idea of appropriacy and to ignore the fact that, whatever can be forced upon pupils in the context of the school, no one register in real life can serve as an all-purpose model.

This leads us to examine a selection of the recommendations concerned with stressing flexibility and a wide range of uses for language in both spoken and written forms.

4 The pupil should be helped to develop increasing technical control over his language so that he can put it to increasingly complex uses.

39 Many young children do not have the opportunity to develop at home the more complex forms of language which school education demands of them. All children should be helped to acquire as wide a range as possible of the uses of language.

110 Children should be helped to as wide as possible

range of language uses so that they can speak appropriately in different situations and use standard forms when they are needed.

127   Pupils should be given the opportunity to write for a variety of readers and audiences. They should be faced with the need to analyse the specific task, to choose the language appropriate to it, and to establish criteria by which to judge what they have achieved.

Here, again, is support for the notion that repertoire range is perhaps the most useful concept for teachers both in aiding their own understanding of language and in any attempts to promote its development. What is being stressed is that teachers can and should accept whatever language variety a child has developed in relation to his background (which includes social, cultural and interest factors), because in the situation in which it has been acquired it works well enough to be deemed adequate and therefore appropriate. But, if equal educational opportunity for all is to have any meaning, then in language experience as well as any other kind of experience pupils must be given opportunities and, indeed, positively helped to acquire the varieties they will need to make sense of their learning.

Probably the most effective methods of doing this will start with making them aware that varieties exist. Some teachers of English will be familiar with a language course that attempts to do this—namely, G. Thornton *et al.*, *Language in Use* (1971). In the present writer's experience, teachers who use this material in the teaching of English language speak highly of it, while warning that it is pitched at a relatively advanced level and assumes a secure foundation of basic language development. Surely it is not an impossible task to produce similar material aimed at less advanced levels? Ideally, such schemes would be able to take account of pupils with average and below-average ability. Schemes of this kind, although run by the English department in a school, could be consciously reinforced in subject departments through the provision of real examples for pupils to work on. The latter point is important, as attempts to teach language skills apart from the need to use them to facilitate understanding and communication in a *real* situation run the risk that what is taught will not be transferred to the real situation.

If promotion in the pupil of an adequately wide repertoire range becomes the major objective of a language programme across the curriculum, it will be necessary for teachers themselves to become acquainted with the characteristics of subject registers other than their own and familiar with the characteristics of their own subject register. They will also need to identify potentially difficult structures, bearing in mind the language competence of individual pupils. It is unlikely that they will be able to do this without acquiring a rudimentary knowledge of language structure and function.

Finally, a look at a selection of recommendations associated with the manner in which language and learning competence grows and with methods for encouraging such growth.

3 Language competence grows incrementally through an interaction of writing, talk, reading and experience and the best teaching deliberately influences the nature and quality of this growth.

36 Language has a unique role in developing human learning: the higher processes of thinking are normally achieved by the interaction of a child's language behaviour with his other mental and perceptual powers.

38 The surest means by which a child is enabled to master his mother tongue is by exploiting the process of discovery through language in all its uses.

112 A stimulating classroom environment will not necessarily of itself develop the children's ability to use language as an instrument for learning. The teacher has a vital part to play and his role should be one of planned intervention.

128 Competence in language comes above all through its purposeful use, not through the working of exercises divorced from context.

The above recommendations are clearly based upon the conclusion that language competence grows naturally through a range of experiences and individual encounters that stimulate language behaviour. But, because experiences, opportunities and abilities vary from one individual to another, the stimulation and promotion of language in all its forms is necessary and desirable. Thus, listening, talking, reading and writing are all part of the language behaviour which is susceptible to the intervention programmes mentioned in the report's recommendations.

It is reassuring to note that listening is included in the list, but the difficulty of this activity is often underestimated, although it plays an important part in learning and language development. Pupils listen with greater attention when they know that they will be expected to respond or react to the message being communicated. Thus, primary and secondary teachers can encourage listening by incorporating in their lessons different kinds of stimuli for this purpose. These may include recalling fact, expressing opinions, recounting the sequence of events, remembering concrete facts, analysing specific factors and evaluating on the basis of information provided in the message. Activities of this sort should do more than increase attentiveness; they should also stimulate different kinds of speech.

Talk has been given much prominence in the recommendations, and there is a strong call for teachers to create situations in which children have to use spoken language with which to explore, recall, predict, plan and analyse. Particular stress is placed on the value of exploratory talk which enables the pupil to think aloud. It is also a preliminary to the acquisition of specialised language, since unfamiliar structures have to be tested if they are to be perfected. In this respect teachers need to know how to exploit experiences and situations with a view to eliciting predictable language responses. Very little of this has been done in the past, perhaps because of a pre-occupation with self-expression, creativity and the like. Teachers should also use the talk sessions in which pupils are reformulating in their own words the steps of a solution to a problem or the logical sequence of an argument to provide themselves with feedback on how successful their teaching has been or to indicate how pupils are progressing with their attempts to use appropriate language.

All secondary teachers also have a role to play in assisting their pupils to master the reading required in their subject area of the school curriculum. It follows, therefore, that they will need to know something about levels of reading difficulty, concept density and use of specialised language in the texts in use. They will also need to understand some of the techniques which are used to improve reading in relation to promoting the efficiency of a pupil's learning—for example, note-taking from texts, discrimination of literal and inferential comprehension, evaluative reading and so on.

The report also clearly recognises that within the possible range of writing there will and should be contexts which are vastly different from one another calling for corresponding skills which are themselves quite distinctive. It should also be stressed that writing is linguistically distinct from speech, and teachers should regard it as another medium for language behaviour and not just as 'talk' put down on paper. Nor should its usefulness be underestimated in promoting reading and spelling skills through the impact upon the pupil's memory of both visual and tactile stimuli.

To sum up, the implicit and explicit message of the conclusions and recommendations of the Bullock Committee have to do with range and variety of language allied to the functions it will have to perform in meeting the demands of different kinds of learning and of everyday life in our particular culture. Although the implications of the recommendations will be open to interpretation, and there will be considerable variation in this respect, there is no support in the report for extreme lines that promote one kind of language at the expense of others, or that see one language variety as intrinsically better than another. Thus, while not confusing children with premature use of technical terms and complicated syntax, it is considered necessary to provide an adequate range of models from which children can derive their own sense of appropriateness. To this end teachers are asked to provide children with opportunities to share personal interests and learning discoveries and problems, take the verbal initiative, listen to one another, solve through discussion together difficulties that arise, make sense of information received from the teaching and books, write and talk in a variety of styles, come to terms with the distinctive mode of analysis of subjects in the curriculum and their linguistic characteristics, and meet varied levels of difficulty and style in written material. There will be practical difficulties associated with attempts to launch language programmes of the scale called for, but such attempts can be justified in the light of the knowledge that language and learning go hand in hand, and a child's social and intellectual growth is contingent upon his mastering *language*.

Bibliography

Arnold, H. (1972), 'Children's conversations, their form and function', unpublished dissertation for the degree of MA (Educ.), University of London Institute of Education.

Bar-Adon, A. and Leopold, W. F. (1971), *Child Language: A Book of Readings*, Englewood Cliffs, NJ: Prentice-Hall.

Barber, C. L. (1962), 'Contributions to English syntax and philology', in Behre, F. (ed.), *Gothenburg Studies in English*, Acta Universitatis Gotoburgensis.

Barnes, D. *et al.* (1969), *Language, the Learner and the School*, Harmondsworth: Penguin Books.

Barnes, D. (1971), 'Classroom contexts for language and learning', in Wilkinson, A. M. (ed.), *The Context of Language, Educational Review*, vol. 23, no. 3, University of Birmingham School of Education.

Barnes, D. (1972) 'Language and learning in the classroom', in *Language in Education, A source book*. Open University/ Routledge & Kegan Paul.

Barnes, D. (1973), *Language in the Classroom*, E. 262, Block 4, Open University.

Barnes, D. (1976), *From Communication to Curriculum*, Harmondsworth: Penguin Books.

Bernstein, B. (1965), 'A sociolinguistic approach to social learning', in Gould, J. (ed.), *Penguin Survey of the Social Sciences 1965*, Harmondsworth: Penguin Books.

Bernstein, B. (1971), *Class, Codes and Control*, Vol. 1, *Theoretical Studies Towards a Sociology of Language*, Routledge & Kegan Paul.

Bernstein, B. (1972*a*), 'Social class, language and socialization', in Giglioli, P. (ed.), *Language and Social Context*, Harmondsworth: Penguin Books.

Bernstein, B. (1972*b*), 'A sociolinguistic approach to socialization with some reference to educability', in Gumperz, J. J. and Hymes, D. H. (eds.), *Directions in Sociolinguistics*, New York: Holt, Rinehart & Winston.

Bernstein, B. (1972*c*), *Class, Codes and Control*, Vol. 2, *Applied Studies in the Sociology of Language*, Routledge & Kegan Paul.

Biddulph, G. M. R. (1963), 'The scientific register', unpublished dissertation for the Diploma of Applied Linguistics, University of Edinburgh.

Bloomfield, L. (1947), 'Linguistic aspects of science', *International Encyclopedia of Unified Science,* vol. 1, no. 4, The University of Chicago Press.

Brandis, W. and Henderson, D. (1970), *Social Class, Language and Communication,* Routledge & Kegan Paul.

Britton, J. N. (1970), *Language and Learning,* Allen Lane.

Britton, J. (1971), 'What's the use?', in Wilkinson, A. M. (ed.), *The Context of Language, Educational Review,* vol. 23, no. 3, University of Birmingham School of Education.

Brown, R. W. (1956), 'Language and categories', appendix in Bruner, J. S. *et al., A Study of Thinking,* New York: Wiley.

Brown, R. W. (1958), *Words and Things,* Free Press of Glencoe.

Brown, R. W. and Lenneberg, E. H. (1961), 'A study in language and cognition', in Saporta, S. (ed.), *Psycholinguistics—a Book of Readings,* New York: Holt, Rinehart & Winston.

Bruner, J. S. (1966), *Towards a Theory of Instruction,* Harvard University Press.

Bullock Report (1974), *A Language for Life,* HMSO.

Burroughs, G. E. R. (1957), *A Study of the Vocabulary of Young Children,* Edinburgh: Oliver & Boyd.

Carroll, J. B. (1964), *Language and Thought,* Foundation of Modern Psychology Series, Englewood Cliffs, NJ: Prentice-Hall.

Carroll, J. B. (1970), 'Words, meanings and concepts', in Stones, E. (ed.), *Readings in Educational Psychology,* Methuen.

Cazden, C. B. (1971), 'Environmental assistance to the child's acquisition of grammar', in Menyuk, P. (ed.), *The Acquisition and Development of Language,* Englewood Cliffs, NJ: Prentice-Hall.

Cazden, C. B., Hymes, D. and John, V. P. (1972), *Functions of Language in the Classroom,* New York and London: Teachers' College Press, Teachers' College, Columbia University.

Coulthard, M. (1969), 'A discussion of restricted and elaborated codes', in Wilkinson, A. M. (ed.), *The State of Language, Educational Review,* vol. 22, no. 1, University of Birmingham School of Education.

Creber, P. (1972), *Lost for Words. Language and Educational Failure,* Harmondsworth: Penguin Books.

Davies, A. (1969), 'The notion of register', in Wilkinson, A. M.

(ed.), *The State of Language, Educational Review,* vol. 22, no. 1, University of Birmingham School of Education.

Doughty, P., Pearce, J., Thornton, G. (1971), *Language in Use,* Schools Council Programme in Linguistics and English Teaching, Edward Arnold.

Esland, G. (1973), *Language and Social Reality,* E 262, Block 2, Open Univesity.

Ervin-Tripp, S. M. (1968), 'An analysis of the interaction of language, topic and listener', in Fishman, J. A. (ed.), *Readings in the Sociology of Language,* The Hague: Mouton.

Evans, J. D. (1972), 'A study of the relationship of the technical vocabulary of selected school text books on the development of scientific concepts in human biology', unpublished thesis for the degree of PhD, University of Cardiff.

Fishman, J. A. (1970), *Sociolinguistics—A Brief Introduction,* Rowley, Massachusetts: Newbury House.

Fishman, J. A. (1972*a*), 'The sociology of language', in Giglioli, P. P. (ed.), *Language and Social Context,* Harmondsworth: Penguin Books.

Fishman, J. A. (1972*b*), 'Domains between macro and micro-sociolinguistics', in Gumperz, J. J. and Hymes, D. H. (eds), *Directions in Sociolinguistics,* New York: Holt, Rinehart & Winston.

Gal'perin, P. Ia. (1970), 'An experimental study in the formation of mental actions', in Stones, E. (ed.), *Readings in Educational Psychology,* Methuen.

Garwood, C. G. (1963), 'The examination of certain linguistic structures contained in chemistry text books used in courses for GCE', unpublished dissertation for the degree of MA, University of London Institute of Education.

Giglioli, P. P. (ed.) (1972), *Language and Social Context,* Harmondsworth: Penguin Books.

Ginsburg, M. (1972), *The Myth of the Deprived Child,* Englewood Cliffs, NJ: Prentice-Hall.

Goldman-Eisler (1961), 'Hesitation and information in speed', in Cherry, C. (ed.), *Information Theory, Fourth London Symposium,* Butterworth.

Goldman-Eisler (1965), 'The common value of pausing time in spontaneous speech', in *Quarterly Journal of Experimental Psychology,* vol. 17.

Gould, J. (ed.) (1965), *Penguin Survey of the Social Sciences,* Harmondsworth: Penguin Books.

Gregory, M. (1967), 'Aspects of varieties differentiation', from *Journal of Linguistics,* vol. 3, no. 2, pp. 177-274.

Gumperz, J. J. and Hymes, D. (1972), *Directions in Sociolinguistics. The Ethnography of Communication,* New York: Holt, Rinehart & Winston.

Halliday, M. A. K., McIntosh, A. and Strevens, P. (1964), *The Linguistic Sciences and Language Teaching,* Longman.

Halliday, M. A. K. (1968), 'Language and experience', in Wilkinson, A. M. (ed.), *The Place of Language, Educational Review,* vol. 20, no. 2, University of Birmingham School of Education.

Halliday, M. A. K. (1969), 'Relevant models of language', in Wilkinson, A. M. (ed.), *The State of Language,* vol. 20, no. 1, University of Birmingham School of Education.

Halliday, M. A. K. (1971), 'Language in a social perspective', in Wilkinson, A. M. (ed.), *The Context of Language, Educational Review,* vol. 23, no. 3, University of Birmingham School of Education.

Hasan, R. (1972), 'Code, register and social dialect' in Bernstein, B. (ed.), *Class, Codes and Control,* Vol. 2, *Applied Studies in the Sociology of Language,* Routledge & Kegan Paul.

Herriot, P. (1971), *Language and Teaching, A Psychological View,* Methuen.

Hoghughi, M. S. (ed.) (1966), *Language and Behaviour—A Symposium,* Aycliffe School.

Johnson, D. M. and O'Reilly, C. A. (1964), 'Concept attainment in children: classifying and defining', *Journal of Educational Psychology,* vol. 55, no. 2, pp. 71-4.

Katz, J. and Fodod, J. (1963), 'The structure of a semantic theory', in *Language,* vol. 39, pp. 70-210.

Klausmeier, H. J. and Harris, C. W. (1966), *Analysis of Concept Learning,* Academic Press.

Labov, W. (1968), 'The reflection of social processes in linguistic structure', in Fishman, J. (ed.), *Readings in the Sociology of Language,* The Hague: Mouton.

Labov, W. (1972), 'The Logic of Nonstandard English', in Giglioli, P. (ed.), *Language and Social Context,* Harmondsworth: Penguin Books.

Lado, R. (1957), *Linguistics across Cultures. Applied Linguistics for Language Teachers,* Ann Arbor: University of Michigan Press.

Lawton, D. (1968), *Social Class, Language and Education,* Routledge & Kegan Paul.

Leech, G. N. (1966), *English in Advertising,* Longman.

Lenneberg, E. H. (1967), *Biological Foundations of Language,* New York: Wiley.

Leong, C. T. (1960), 'An examination of certain linguistic features in text books on physics up to GCE "O" level', unpublished thesis for the degree of MA, University of London Institute of Education.

Loban, W. (1963), 'The language of elementary school children', in *National Council of Teachers of English Campaign 111. Research Report 1.*

Luria, A. R. and Yudovich, I. (1970), 'Language and mental development', in Stones, E. (ed.), *Readings in Educational Psychology,* Methuen.

Manis, M. (1971), *An Introduction to Cognitive Psychology,* Belmont, California: Brooks/Cole Publishing Co.; Wadsworth Publishing Co.

Menyuk, P. (1971), *Acquisition and Development of Language,* Hemel Hempstead: Prentice-Hall.

McIntosh, A. and Halliday, M. A. K. (1966), *Patterns of Language. Papers in General, Descriptive and Applied Linguistics,* Longman.

Natadze, R. G. (1970), 'The mastery of scientific concepts in school', in Stones, E. (ed.), *Readings in Educational Psychology,* Methuen.

Nisbet, R. (1973), 'Poetry and permissiveness', in *AMA Journal,* November 1973, pp 197-8.

O'Donnell, W. R. (1967), *An Investigation into the Role of Language in a Physics Examination,* Moray House College of Education, Edinburgh.

Opie, I. and P. (1959), *The Lore and Language of Schoolchildren,* Oxford University Press.

Peel, E. A. (1970), 'Some problems in the psychology of history teaching: Historical ideas and concepts', in Stones, E. (ed.), *Readings in Educational Psychology,* Methuen.

Powers, S. R. (1926), *Important Terms Compiled from Textbooks for General Science, Biology, Physics and Chemistry,* Columbia University, New York Teachers' College.

Pressey, L. C. (1924), 'The determination of the technical vocabulary of the school subjects', *School and Society*, vol. XX, no. 499, pp. 95-6.

Richards, J. W. (1971), 'A comparative study of the effectiveness of three methods of teaching biology', unpublished exercise submitted in partial fulfilment of the requirement for the Diploma in Advanced Educational Studies, University of Newcastle-upon-Tyne.

Richards, J. W. (1974), 'The language of biology teaching', unpublished thesis for the degree of M.Ed, University of Newcastle-upon-Tyne.

Robinson, W. P. (1965a), 'Cloze procedure as a technique for the investigation of social class differences in language usage', in *Language and Speech,* vol. 8, pp. 42-55.

Robinson, W. P. (1965b), 'The elaborated code in working class language', in *Language and Speech,* vol. 8, pp. 243-52.

Robinson, W. P. (1972), *Language and Social Behaviour,* Harmondsworth: Penguin Books.

Rosen, H. (1969), 'An investigation of the effects of differentiated writing assignments on the performance in English composition of a selected group of 15/16 year old pupils', unpublished thesis for the degree of PhD, University of London.

Rosen, H. (1972), *Language and Class: A Critical Look at the Theories of Basil Bernstein,* Fallingwall Press.

Sapir, E. (1970), 'Language and concepts', in Stones, E. (ed.), *Readings in Educational Psychology,* Methuen.

Saporta, S. (ed.), *Psycholinguistics—A Book of Readings,* New York: Holt, Rinehart & Winston.

Sharp, R. and Green, A. (1975), *Education and Social Control* Routledge & Kegan Paul.

Skemp, R. (1970), 'Concept formation and its significance in mathematics teaching and syllabus reform', in Stones, E. (ed.), *Readings in Educational Psychology,* Methuen.

Spiker, C., Gerjuoy, I. and Shepherd, W. (1956), *Journal of Comparative Psychology,* no. 49, pp 416-19.

Stones, E. (1970), *Readings in Educational Psychology. Learning and Teaching,* Methuen.

Strevens, P. D. (ed.) (1966), *Five Inaugural Lectures,* Language and Language Learning Series, Oxford University Press.

Stringer, D. (1973), *Language Variation and English, E 262,* Block 1, Open University.

Swift, D. F. (1968), 'Social class and educational adaptation', in Butcher, H. S. (ed.), *Educational Research in Britain,* vol. 1, pp. 289-96.

Taylor, G. (1968), 'Language and learning, deep structure in a chemical text', unpublished thesis for the degree of M.Litt, University of Edinburgh.

Thornton, G. *et al.* (1971), *Schools Council Programme in Linguistics and English Teaching,* Edward Arnold.

Ure, J. N. (1969), *Practical Registers in English Language Teaching,* vol. XXIII, no. 2, and vol. XXIII, no. 3.

Vygotsky, L. S. (1962), *Thought and Language,* Cambridge, Massachusetts: Massachusetts Institute of Technology Press.

Westbury I. and Bellack, A. A. (eds) (1971), *Research into Classroom Processes.* New York: Teachers College Press.

Wilkinson, A. M. (ed.) (1969), *The State of Language, Educational Review,* vol. 22, no. 1, University of Birmingham School of Education.

Wilkinson, A. M. (ed.) (1971), *The Context of Language, Educational Review,* vol. 23, no. 3, University of Birmingham School of Education.

Wilkinson, A. M. (1971), *The Foundations of Language. Talking and Reading in Young Children,* Oxford University Press.

Wragg, E. C. (1971), *Analysis of the Verbal Classroom Interaction between Student Teachers and Children,* SSRC Report, University of Exeter Department of Education.

Index

Acquisition: of concepts, *see* concepts, acquisition and development of; of language, *see* language, acquisition and development of

Adequacy, of language 11, 34-5, 43, 52-5, 65, 70, 100, 125-9, 133, 137-9

Appropriacy, of language 35, 41-4, 53, 69-72, 115, 127, 133, 142-3

Barnes, D. 17, 56-62, 71, 75-8, 88, 92, 135

Bernstein, B. 36-45, 48, 49, 52-4, 122

Biddulph, G. 71

Britton, J. 16-19

Brown, R. W. 99

Bruner, J. S. 96-7

Bullock Report 15, 94, 127, 137-41, 143

Carroll, J. B. 99

Chomsky 42

Class: social 10, 36-45, 47-9, 52-6, 121-5; stereotypes 10, 122-5

Codes, linguistic 36-45, 48-9, 52-6

Concepts 14, 20-4, 63-4, 76, 91-2, 94, 97, 101-20, 143; Acquisition and development of 20-1, 95-119, 124-5, 134-9, 144; conceptualisation 37, 100, 104, 135; conceptual levels 60-4, 81, 91-2, 112-15, 118, 134

Context 10, 29, 32-6, 40-4, 51-5, 59-69, 80, 94, 130-39, 143; of situation 16, 32

Coulthard, M. 42, 45

Creativity, nature of 29-35; in language use 32, 65, 142; in writing 30-1, 34-5

Creber, P. 126, 133

Culture 16, 37-9, 49, 52-6, 97, 118-21, 140, 143

Curriculum 9, 37-9

Deep structure 63, 102-4, 136

Deficiency, linguistic 38, 44-5, 48-54

Deprivation, language 45, 49, 124-5

Deviancy of language 46-50, 55, 65, 67; *see also* standard and non-standard English

Dialect 36, 46-56, 68-9; *see also* standard and non-standard English

Dialogue 46, 60, 71, 74-81

Discourse 42-3, 69, 83-94, 104, 130

Doughty, P. 140

Elaborated codes *see* linguistic codes

English, standard and non-standard 46-56, 64-5, 68; scientific English, *see* language of science

Evans, J. D. 63, 104, 136

Expressive language, *see* functions of language

Family 36-8

Fishman, J. D. 10, 43, 94, 123-5

Fodor, S. 32

Functions of language 10-14, 16-21, 24-9, 33-5, 53-9, 62-9, 75-9, 90-8, 113-20, 124, 127, 132-8, 141

Gerjuoy 99

Goldman-Eisler 41-2

Halliday, M. A. K. 16, 18, 32-3, 68, 92, 97

Hasan 32

Hesitation phenomena 41-2

Katz, J. 32

Labov, W. 46-56, 64

Language, nature of 9-10, 12-16, 120, 122-4; acquisition and development of 10-12, 18, 22, 45-6, 95-6, 104-5, 109, 125-7, 131, 138-9; child's own 11, 56, 65, 91; functions of, *see* functions of language; of instruction, *see* learning, language of; normal conversational 35, 47, 59, 64-5, 76, 93-4; practices 12-13, 17-18, 22-5, 34-5, 95, 120-2; of science 43-4, 71, 79, 87, 91-4, 113-16, 134-5; of secondary education 57-62, 71-2, 77, 92, 135; specialised 43, 51, 61-5, 74-7, 89-91,

Language, *cont.*,
95-119, 134-42; stimulation and extension of 21-9, 33-7, 64, 126, 130, 142-3; systems 16, 29, 37, 46, 57, 64, 98, 125-7; of teachers and pupils 56-67, 75, 79, 92, 101-3, 118, 129-35; varieties, *see* varieties of language
Lawton, D. 44
Learning 60-2, 96-7, 100, 115, 130, 133-44; language of subject 13-15, 59-65, 67-94, 103, 119; role of language in 11, 56-60, 63-7, 96, 104, 118, 125, *see also* concept acquisition and development of
Leech, G. N. 70-1, 92; analytic mode of linguistic features of journalism 82-5
Lenneberg, E. H. 125
Lexis 33, 37, 41-2, 48, 65, 70-1, 87
Linguistics 10, 68-9, 85
Linguistic competence 66, 117-18, 134, 141
Listening 131-2
Loban, W. 46

O'Donnell 118

McIntosh, A. 69-70
Meaning 16-18, 28, 32-4, 40-3, 55, 60-6, 98-104, 133-6
Mode of discourse, *see* discourse; of thinking 14, 69
Models, 10, 40, 75, 85, 92, 98, 117, 120-2, 125, 139, 143

Nisbet, R. 27-9

Peel, E. A. 104
Personality factors in relation to communicative climate 122, 128-32
Poetic, *see* functions of language

Questions 58-9, 75-81, 105-8, 113-17; role in classroom dialogue 59, 75, 87, 105-19, 129-30

Reading 46, 48-52, 133, 141-3
Register 59-62, 68-72, 77, 91-4, 104-5, 109, 113-19, 134-6, 141; *see also*

Register, *cont.*,
language varieties; subject register 71, 82-93
Repertoire 10, 43, 56, 65, 93-4, 119, 123-7, 133-41, 143
Restricted code, *see* codes, linguistic
Richards, J. W. 72, 104-18, 129, 136
Role of discourse, *see* discourse
Rosen, H. 52, 54, 57, 61

Self expression 16-29, 142; *see also* functions of language
Shepherd 99
Situation 35, 47, 51-5, 65, 69-70, 124-7, 134, 140-1, *see also* context
Skemp, R. 104
Speech 37-45, 47-56, 69, 72-6, 69-96, 128, 130-6, 140-3; community 43, 48, 52-5, 68-9, 99, 123-7, 141; network 43, 50, 124-5; rate of speaking 41-2
Spiker, C. 99
Strevens, P. D. 70
Style of discourse, *see* discourse
Switching 41, 43-4, 124
Syntax 11, 33, 37, 40-2, 48, 65, 70-1, 102, 116-18, 143

Taylor, G. 63-4, 71, 104, 136
Technical Language, *see* specialised language; term 61-5, 79, 89-91, 101-5, 113-16, 132-6, 143
Thornton, G. 140
Transactional, *see* functions of language

Underachievement 49-52, 54-5
Ure, J. N. 69
User language 13, 36-67, 115

Varieties of language 10, 14, 34-5, 42-4, 50-5, 64-9, 92, 95-8, 115-18, 124-7, 132-40, 143-4; *see also* codes, dialects and registers
Verbal activity 64, 96-100, 103, 117-19, 130, 132, 136
Vygotsky, L. S. 20, 21, 95-8

Writing 69, 87, 92, 140-3

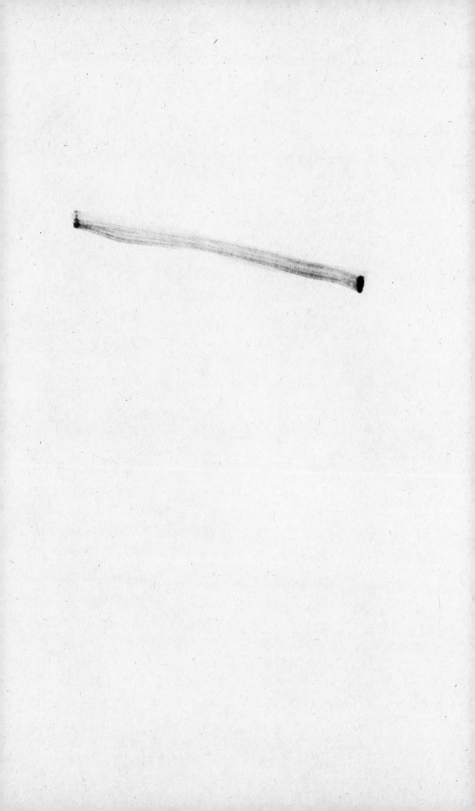